# In the City

# In the City

Random Acts of Awareness

*Colette Brooks*

W. W. NORTON & COMPANY

NEW YORK  LONDON

For information about permission to reproduce selections from this book, write to
Permissions, W. W. Norton & Company, Inc., 500 Fifth Avenue, New York, NY 10110

The text and display of this book are composed in Fairfield
Composition by Adrian Kitzinger
Manufacturing by Quebecor Fairfield
Book design by Lovedog Studios
Production manager: Julia Druskin

Library of Congress Cataloging-in-Publication Data
Brooks, Colette.
  In the city : random acts of awareness / Colette Brooks.—1st ed.
    p. cm.
  **ISBN 0-393-05108-0 (hardcover)**
  1. City and town life. 2. Civilization, Modern. I. Title.
  HT119 .B76 2002
  307.76—dc21

                         2002000519

W. W. Norton & Company, Inc., 500 Fifth Avenue, New York, N.Y. 10110
www.wwnorton.com

W. W. Norton & Company Ltd., Castle House, 75/76 Wells Street, London W1T 3QT

1 2 3 4 5 6 7 8 9 0

*To Charlene and Billy*
*who always hoped to see the city*
*for themselves*

# In the City

*How does the story begin?*

*One possibility: a young girl dreams about a place she's only heard of in books, in movies, on TV. It's much bigger than the town in which she's grown up. People in that distant place are busy, happy, never bored. They wear long dresses that billow as they walk, or tailored suits and hats. They have jobs; some even have careers. They fall in and out of love, which is natural, considering how many other people are always around.*

*Maybe, the girl thinks, there's room for one more.*

*She takes the heavy encyclopedia off the shelf and looks the city up, traces its streets, its neighborhoods, its odd unpronounce-*

*able names. She wonders, ever so hesitantly, what it might be like to live there. And so the mysterious process has begun: the city is reeling her in.*

That's one way the story might start.

What kind of person is a *city person*?

One possibility: the kind of person who doesn't feel the need to finish a jigsaw puzzle, who relishes jagged edges and orphaned curves, stray bits of data, pieces of stories parsed from sentences half overheard on the street.

A person who picks up crumpled sections of newspaper in the streetcar or subway and reads haphazardly until the next stop.

According to recent reports, 7.4 percent of this city's population has declared itself *agnostic*. For them, the essential nature of the world is unknowable; no matter of talk about first causes or higher powers can explain the shape and drift of experience. The remaining 92.6 percent of the populace either knows what's going on, which is unlikely, or cannot bring itself to admit that it's flying in the dark.

It's those others who interest me.

They're the ones who buy the newspaper and try to read it straight through.

What sort of person is drawn to the city?

One possibility: someone beset by the urge to jump off a cliff, or drive into oncoming traffic, or plunge into claustrophobic proximity to legions of similarly antic beings. If you're bold enough you don't think about it, you just do it, and for the duration of the ride the experience is exhilarating.

Some health professionals characterize such thinking as distorted cognition, even suicidal ideation. But it might be simpler to term it *the urban mind-set.*

One gets dizzy just thinking about it.

Who else is drawn to the city?

One possibility: someone who isn't quite sure how he or she got there, doesn't know how it will all come out, but hopes to make the best of it, whatever it ultimately is.

Like the castaway who found himself clinging to a piece of wood, washed up onto shore, having suffered what some would call a *life's shipwreck,* thinking at first that rescue was imminent, not so sure some twenty years later.

He would have been very much at home here.

According to one futurist, science would be better served by studying the dwindling reserves of hunter-gatherers in the world than the residents of cities; urban enclaves are only ten thousand or so years old, much too recent to tell us much about the genetic bearing of human beings.

The urban psyche, in other words, may be of little evolutionary value.

But that's still up in the air, and those of us who wonder have only a few thousand years to sort it all out. Soon, experts predict, a majority of the world's population will have gravitated to urban centers. Rural life as we know it will more or less disappear. A major city will form every three minutes, as if metastasizing, while the planet's natural resources wither away.

What will it take to survive in the city?

With any luck, at least a few of us may find out.

✦　　✦　　✦

Fact: from a distance, she seems adrift in the harbor, her diminutive figure almost fragile, hardly distinguishable from the derricks and spires that crowd the horizon around her. I have seen her countless times, of course, up close in books; there she commands one's attention as if by entitlement. But the living city is less respectful of its residents, and one can ride the train to the city's outer reaches without even noticing her through the window.

I search her out.

I have come to believe that she is not standing in watchful repose but waving, hoping to catch someone's eye, as if she were weary of her solitude and wished ardently to join us. I watch for her upraised arm; I seem to be the only one who sees her. Before the train rounds out of sight, however, I find myself turning away, for such naked expression of need is somehow unseemly.

Each of the streets in the city, they say, has a story. Some of the buildings lining its routes were erected in another century; at times, when I hardly expect it, I turn a corner and the old world rises as if from a vision into view. On one block I see the windows through which scores of young women once leapt to their deaths, fire driving them from factory floor to the cool of the open air, their hair held in place with ribbons of flame as they fell. I know their names: *Jennie, Rose, Rachel, Essie, Annie . . .*

How quiet this place seems now, the screams of that hour followed by years of silence. College students run by without thinking. Sometimes, someone else who remembers places white roses on the sidewalk.

I've heard that one worker, on that long-ago day, lifted some of the women clear of the stone ledge so that they might drop more easily to the hard ground below. After he had done all he could to ease their way he joined them. He seems to have loved one of the girls; in the end, in an act of intimacy beyond his imagining, he found himself bound, forever, to all of them.

As if in recognition of that fact, fourteen engagement rings were later found on the ashen floor.

I would like to have met that young fellow. Sometimes, when the wind picks up, I think of him walking these streets with me, even as a ghost ever watchful.

Fact: in 1851, a woman was struck and killed by an ice cart while crossing a city street. It was surely not the first calamity of its kind here, but it was the first to be noted in the inaugural issue of what has since become our newspaper of record.

Losing her life, I imagine, was the last thing on the woman's mind as she awoke on that mid-nineteenth century morning. She might have felt even worse had she known that news of her misfortune would be proclaimed in such a public fashion. But what is oddest: that one should be in the wrong place at the wrong time, a victim of cruel mischance, or that a stranger should still shake her head at such a fate some 150 years later?

No one here worries much about ice carts any longer. Our newspaper now recounts other oddities—*Human Foot Found in River, Passers-by Lift Car off Woman Pinned Against Wall, Additional Bomb Found in Apartment of Dead Man*—that some of us read as portents, signs of the worst that may come to pass if we're not careful, or maybe even if we are.

It's the kind of reflection that no thoughtful observer need dwell upon. What can you say, once the ominous possibilities have been entertained, except that anything can happen? That one day, given the odds, something of ours might be found floating waywardly in a river?

It's not surprising that those who fear the unexpected take their own superstitious precautions against it. One young cop on the beat keeps objects tucked, like talismans, in the plastic liner of his cap—a memorial card that reads *in loving memory,* a child's tiny drawing splashed with orange, yellow, and red. He holds them close, as if the thin pieces of paper might shield him from harm.

But apprehension weaves its own symbiotic circles in the city, so that those the cops are afraid of fear them, in turn, even more.

The rest of us work to stay alert. It's possible, of course, to lose perspective. After all, no one takes note of the multiple near misses or close calls that must undoubtedly add up in the course of a given day.

But maybe such lack of awareness is a mercy the city extends, like balm from an unknown benefactor, never expecting thanks.

The young, it seems, have long been considered at special risk in the city. Years ago, those who were more experienced attempted to shield children from the melancholia of city life.

*Handwritten charms to stop children from crying were sometimes taped to lampposts,* our official encyclopedia tells us. We don't have such able remedies today, just an increasing collection of anxieties.

From a recent edition of the newspaper: *Boy, 4, Found Alone on Street.*

Which is scarier: to be sad surrounded by others, or to be sad all by yourself?

✦     ✦     ✦

Years ago, when I first came upon this place, it seemed to me nothing but noise, an unremitting roar. Now, especially at night, I can distinguish the varying pitch of the city's sounds: the mechanical alarms that wail, stricken, crying out to one another in contagion; the low intermittent rumbles in subterranean cavities; the dull pops on the street that seem to come in clusters. Sometimes, it really is a car that's backfiring.

Occasionally, in the morning, the delicate sounds of small birds cut through the aural clutter. For a moment the city becomes the country. It's unsettling, a confusion of contexts.

But invariably the birds begin to work themselves up, as if they too are disoriented, on the edge of agitation. They seem to quiet down once the traffic picks up, sirens sound, and the city reasserts itself.

Or maybe I just can't hear them anymore.

Have I spoken yet of solitude? If so, I was mistaken, for almost no one is truly alone here. As I move from one district to another, for example, I encounter a succession of former selves. Some of them seem almost like strangers.

As the years pass, I find myself more easily spooked than ever.

It's the same with the city. Look at the old photographs: women in long skirts and parasols, men in bowler hats, horses loping along streets with familiar names that seem almost unrecognizable.

Or the drawings, even older: scattered wooden buildings surrounded by wilderness, space almost aching in its emptiness and expectation.

Some people think this place has no memory, is always starting over. But I don't see it that way.

The city has always been burdened, even haunted, by its history. The city has never been new.

Does the city read anything besides newspapers?

One young man, too little to read on his own, is listening to a story being recited aloud by his mother. They're both standing in a crowded subway car at rush hour. The story revolves around a little house that finds itself in a city, bullied by the tall buildings that have sprouted up all around it. The woman is having some trouble balancing the book in her free hand, but she pushes on, telling her son about the Good Samaritan who wants to tow the little house back to the open land where it belongs. At the close of the story, in its last picture, the house is seen smiling as it ambles down a country road.

*Never again would she be curious about the city. Never again would she want to live there.*

The two arrive at their stop; the woman closes the book and rushes the boy out the door. As I watch them leave, I wonder: was that a happy ending?

Fact: one city woman, a cook by trade, lent her name long ago to the most fearsome disease of her day. It seems that she served the illness up with each meal she prepared for others but didn't seem to suffer from the malady herself.

The first few times they tracked her down she refused to be treated. But she wanted to be left alone, so she pledged to find some other way to support herself.

How could they know she would adopt a false name and keep on with her lethal work?

It seems she never thought to leave the city. The outbreaks continued. She became famous, after a fashion. Children sang songs in the streets about her; newspapers featured her deadly countenance in cartoons.

One day, after some time, they found her once again. She was forcibly confined to an island in the harbor for the remaining twenty-some years of her life. Though she was considered a guest of the city, she was said to be ungrateful, even surly.

Maybe she just hadn't envisioned things working out that way.

I have a theory: I believe that this story can actually be considered a case study of the city, of its power, of how it can hold you, seize on something inside you, draw you into its orbit even when you have a thousand chances to get away.

Call it *the epidemiology of the urban condition*.

Most of the time, you feel fine. You work, play, appear willingly in public, talk to strangers, make idle plans for the future. You're used to the rush, the edge, you may even think you need it. Your blind resolve is infectious.

But one day you begin to suspect that there might be another way of living, another kind of life. By then, however, it is often too late to start yet another story.

*Besides, it can't hurt to stick around just a little while longer.*

That's when you know the city has hooked you. Eventually, over time, you come to realize that you're even more ill than you thought, for you simply cannot conceive of your life having worked out in any other way.

What else is the city reading?

One young Latino in a bookstore, arms tight in a T-shirt, riffs through *Self-Destructive Behaviors*, oblivious to the ongoing commotion around him. Other readers: a man on the subway, where most of the city's reading is done, carefully working his way through a xeroxed pamphlet entitled *Safety Training*; two young women, one parsing *Good and Evil,* the other *Vocabulary Building for the College-Bound*; an older woman reading and rereading a single page of *HTML for Dummies*; the middle-aged Indian whose eyes never leave the *Complete Works of Swami Vivekananda,* no matter how the train pitches and rolls as it thunders on; a young Spanish woman gripping an outsized book with large print and colorful pictures, underlining passages with pen and ruler, highlighting the words *Mialgro* and *Jesus* with a yellow marker; a Hasid reading the Talmud, its tiny black and white figures unfolding in intricate patterns across the page.

Some aren't reading at all, like the young woman who holds tightly on to *Help for Shy People,* her eyes darting from face to face as if she's afraid that someone might speak. Or the disheveled woman who struts up and down the car, her voice breaking off into growls and barks, who falls silent as she spies the torn copy of *Labor and Monopoly Capital* on the floor and gives it several violent kicks, sending it into a series of spirals, the book's spine finally splitting so that it breaks apart, at which point she turns away.

Each of these city dwellers is studying for something. But the one who may learn the most, I suspect, is a young woman who has recently decided, on a whim, to read only the books that she sees others reading at random. Though she is working her way through a degree-granting institution, this course in the arbitrary that she pursues in her spare time may be the most valuable of all. For what better way to live in the city than to surrender, unresisting, to its rhythms?

If nothing else, she is preparing herself for a lifetime of learning.

✦        ✦        ✦

At any given moment, much of the city is lost or missing, or so it seems from the signs that appear as its citizens appeal for attention. This is how the city speaks to itself—strangers post homemade fliers on telephone poles, bulletin boards, sides of buildings, storefronts, or the slapdash wooden fences that flank construction sites. Sometimes, the signs are done in careful block letters, sometimes in cursive script that reveals, in its wild loops and curls, unmistakable signs of distress.

*Lost, found, lost, found,* the mournful pattern repeats itself.

For every instance of exhilaration (*Young Miniature Poodle Found—Encontramos un Poodle Pequeno*) a new sorrow erupts for someone else (*Lost Bird—grey and white cockatiel last seen at Waverly & 6th!*).

Sometimes, it's the less tangible pieces of one's life that one loses:

MISSING ART WORK
Reward, no questions asked
It means so much to me as an artist!

Occasionally, a single shoe is marooned in the city, like the blue plastic beach sandal, adult-sized, that lies on a much-traveled summer sidewalk, the crowd making a careful circuit around it. Or the woman's dress pump that lands, askew, not far from something covered by a sheet next to a fire hydrant. The shoe seems to be posing, if reluctantly, for the picture that appears the next day in the paper. It is captioned *A Lonely Ending.*

Sometimes, one sees the moment of severance itself play out before one's eyes. A woman leaves the subway in a state of distraction. She realizes, as if awakening, that she has left her package behind. She turns back. Passengers attempt to pass it to her as she reaches out, but it's too late, the doors close.

The package, orphaned, hurtles on without her.

Sometimes, of course, it's people who are lost.

*Missing: Girl, age 16, height 5'7", 135 lbs., eyes & hair dark brown.*

Sometimes there are names, sometimes pictures on the posters. The subject is usually smiling, as if nothing like this could ever happen, as if no life could be thrown so inexplicably off course.

Every day there are more signs of the missing: another sixteen-year-old girl, a twenty-one-year-old boy *last seen on March 11.*

Meanwhile the city, as always, remains alert, ever on the lookout for these lost parts of itself.

In one old book I have read of a land where texts would appear, letter by letter, in the dialect most familiar to the reader, so that the same book could be understood by a multitude of strangers who lacked a common language.

What an odd thought: *no translation necessary.*

Merchants in this foreign place traded not in gold, silk, or silver but in the more ethereal commodity we have come to call *information.*

They likened such knowledge to light.

It's appealing, this idea, the unknown stripped, layer by layer, to a state of complete transparency. It offers an antidote to all that is dark, clouded, and difficult to decipher, to the natural state of the city.

✦     ✦     ✦

That ancient mode of exchange is in some ways familiar to us, for here we also value information. For instance, there's money to be had for *information leading to the arrest and indictment* of those responsible for the explosion that occurred outside a deserted office building at 5:50 A.M. on last November 9.

The known facts have been laid out on a flier: *Call this number, you don't have to give your name.* It's posted haphazardly, as if it won't be up there very long.

Many city people know a little, a few lucky ones know a lot.

*I know because I've been there,* a man on the street declaims to the world at large, his arms chopping the air.

*I knew it right away from his face,* a woman whispers to a companion.

*I see where it's at, I see what's happening,* yet another seer mutters, mostly to himself.

But some are fated to remain befuddled, like the middle-aged man who's speaking to a friend. He's been telling a story, but it isn't going well.

*I said, "What do you mean?"*

*And he said, "You know what I mean."*

At that the speaker pauses, searching his friend's face. Then he falls silent, as if even now he can't understand just where he went wrong.

For those who have lost their way entirely in the city there are consolations, like those conveyed in the words *Christo Salva* that are emblazoned, as if for solace, on a yellow neon cross that shines out from a city rooftop. Like most such signs it dims in the daylight, when darkness doesn't seem quite so overwhelming.

✦       ✦       ✦

Fact: someone has stolen almost six hundred books from a celebrated university library.

There are still four million other volumes in the prestigious
stacks, an ample supply of reading material, but the theft of
accumulated thought on such a scale has proven especially
disturbing.

The university librarians, experts in such matters, have
deemed the works in question *irreplaceable*. We know so little,
after all, and the loss of so many books raises the worrisome
specter of our knowing even less.

The suspect is a man in his mid-forties, no longer affiliated
with the university, but a perennial student even so. It seems
he was something of a philosopher. The three purloined titles
named in the newspaper indicate an interest in arcane thinking of the sixteenth century.

But we know nothing of the 567 or so other titles that he took.

Who can say what he was really ruminating upon in his dark
apartment?

Someone else, it seems, has used a razor to cut old maps out of
an ancient atlas stored in yet another university repository,
leaving a series of holes in its painstakingly rendered pages.

Apparently there's a market for such antiquities, for these
fragile sheets of paper upon which someone long ago inked in
the limits of the known world.

In this case, the felon has been apprehended but the maps
have disappeared. The presiding judge, at the sentencing, talks
of the *loss to history* that the theft represents.

Someone has to speak for the missing parts of the puzzle.

✦       ✦       ✦

Fact: this is the city that produced the country's first master showman, a name now synonymous with con artistry and, to a lesser extent, the circus. He was an early proponent of the freak show, a mode of presentation that he almost single-handedly brought into being.

He collected unnatural specimens of all sorts in his museum. Strange dogs, mutant livestock, mustachioed women, tiny men, and other improbable creatures were displayed in curious clumps.

In this collection of *living curiosities* he placed scale models of nineteenth century world cities—Paris, Dublin, Jerusalem— as if to suggest that the city itself would be the sideshow of the future, the place where the truly odd ones would one day convene of their own accord.

We have a miniature version of our own city on permanent display in the slightly seedy remains of what was once a grand exhibition. But few people now visit the 895,000 tiny structures built to scale, the city within a city that mirrors in its angles and curves the exact topography of its parent.

One can see little bridges, little blocklike buildings, tiny cylindrical water towers, a child-sized city laid out in wood and plastic.

It's the world's largest such simulacrum.

The setup is eerily similar to what one sees from the observation deck of what was once the world's tallest building and still reigns as its eighth wonder. From that height, on the ribbon of street below, tiny yellow cabs disgorge little stick people who turn into teeny pedestrians, bent upon itsy-bitsy errands and encounters.

From this perspective multiple scenarios suggest themselves for each move and feint on the ground.

Is the ant-sized person who's running across the street late for an appointment, or is she being pursued? Will the oncoming toy cars slow down or will they accelerate when they finally see her?

The city has always been half imagined.

Early in another century, when settlers still confined themselves to the tip of the island and rarely ventured into the wilderness beyond, the streets to come were laid out in hypothetical rows of rectangular boxes, the island subdivided into blocks, cross streets, and avenues. It was a vision of order set out in a grand design. Three streets a year were settled in that era as the city slowly grew into itself, and fantasy became fact.

Today one artist, a city employee, also works in miniature, rendering models of crime scenes for the authorities, painstakingly constructing tiny subway platforms, stores with toy cash registers and counters, short streets on which midget police cars are parked at crazy angles, stubby street lamps providing just a little light. The sites are reconstructed with a jeweler's care and precision. But criminal and victim are missing in these models.

Some things, it seems, can't be imagined at all.

In a disaster movie I once watched that landmark building tilt sideways until it toppled, great clouds of dust rising from the simulated crush of stone. The real thing took seven million man-hours to build; the movie version came down in less than a minute.

It's all a question of scale.

I sometimes wonder what it would be like to walk around in

our tiny model city, one foot hovering over a whole city block. I would, of course, be careful, lest I crush something that could not easily be recreated.

One day, on the street, I hear a partial description of a suspect coming in over a policeman's radio as I pass: *White T-shirt, blue pants.* At least I presume it's a suspect. And, for that matter, a description. The cops begin to swivel around, eyeing the crowds, and I start looking too, looking for someone who might be young, might be male, wearing an outfit that has suddenly become suspect itself. But there are more white T-shirts and blue pants here than I can keep track of. Several possibles walk by, brazenly; they seem almost to saunter as they undergo the inspection of the two in the blue shirts, blue pants, black shoes.

I am suddenly reminded of the time I needed to find a particular clerk in a store. I wasn't getting anywhere with a general approach. I decided to refine my description: *The one with the bad rug.* The obdurate salesman nodded. *That's Bob.* And off he went to get Bob.

The city is teeming with white T-shirts, blue pants, black shoes, bad rugs. Also blue shirts, gray slacks, short skirts. Most of the time that's all we see of the myriad strangers we pass, and most of the time that's enough.

Recently, in a neighborhood I had once lived in, I saw a face staring at me from a poster attached to a light pole. Or rather staring past me, in the oddly impersonal manner of such sketches. *Wanted for murder: Male, white, 38–42, 5' 9" to 6', sandy blond hair thinning on top.* He is wearing glasses in the simple line drawing, this man who is losing his hair, who stands accused of a crime I can only intermittently conceive of committing, whose likeness has now become the latest addition to our growing urban portrait gallery.

I probably never saw him while I lived in this area. But now I have one more face on the street to watch out for.

Fact: someone in an apartment high on an upper floor is looking out at the city from a window, idly, in the dead of winter. Her gaze moves from the view to the book she is lazily skimming and back again. Sudden movement from the apartments across the way catches her eye, she looks out, and before she can even cry out she sees a neighbor she will never know rush through her open balcony door and leap right over the railing.

It happens so suddenly, the witness thinks she almost imagined it.

For a year or so to come, she'll tell a few others about that moment, the one she simply can't shake. In this way she will pass the picture on to other people, who will nod their heads as they imagine it, wondering, solemnly, *just what are the odds of that?*

Sometimes now I too see the woman as she leaps into her inadvertent arabesque, her white nightgown melting into the soft light snow on the street. Soon enough a crowd will gather, strangers will gape from a distance, cars with sharp piercing sirens will assemble, the city will respond to and absorb yet another injury to its very being.

But in that moment before she's identified in official jargon as a *jumper*, or declared *dead* by the medical examiner, she lies in limbo.

And those of us who never knew her watch the spectacular fall, over and over again.

✦　　✦　　✦

Occasionally, people get pushed into action, the decision is made for them, as with the young woman who lived just three years in the city before a man described as deranged shoved her into the path of a subway train.

She was killed instantly.

The city itself is subsequently depicted as *on edge* in a wire story that makes its way around the country. For a time, fear of chance seems to snake through the streets.

The young woman's dreams and aspirations are documented at length in press coverage over succeeding days, as the shock of the story spreads.

*She loved the city,* her stricken family reminds itself.

In thousands of homes, bars, and hotels the odds against calamity are cautiously recalculated. Most agree: *it's a million to one.*

Eventually, the shaken city recovers its composure and the woman's hopes are passed on, without ceremony, to somebody else.

*So who is telling the story?*

*I suppose it makes sense to say that I am telling the story, reflecting on my limited experience and willing it into something larger, working assiduously from one small piece of the puzzle.*

*But wait. That doesn't really seem right. I can hardly hope to speak for millions I've never met; I can sometimes hardly speak for myself.*

*Here's a thought: maybe it's the city that's telling the story. Why not? It's been around a lot longer than I have, you might say it's seen it all, what better qualification than such intimate acquaintance?*

*And yet that's not quite right either. The city is pridefully dark, cryptic, it seems almost to have a vested interest in its own opacity. What would remain of its power if its mystique were so easily explained away?*

*No, the answer must lie elsewhere. What's left, once the city and its subjects fall silent? Which voice persists, like an ancient, faltering life-form, unwilling to expire?*

*Who is telling the story?*

*Maybe the story is telling itself.*

Fact: Almost forty million phone calls are made each day in the city, more and more of them conducted (it would seem) on the street. Lately, the city seems to be overrun with people speaking to unseen others, their conversations cast like invisible threads across the brick and concrete chasms.

It seems as if only the truly marginal are still tethered to a phone booth.

On one afternoon, at least three of the forty million calls are made simultaneously by young men in suits scurrying along an east-side street, juggling cell phones and briefcases in their free arms. At that moment, far above them, on an upper floor of a renowned building of burnished bronze designed by Mies van der Rohe, an older man, jacket tossed aside, stands loosely cradling a phone as he looks out at the scene below, his lean body framed by the thin bronze bands of the elegant full-length window.

He seems relaxed, as if unconcerned about the anxious scramble beneath him.

But not everyone has arrived, as it happens, and many still only aspire to windows and upper floors.

*I wasn't able to schmooze my way into it,* a young man farther downtown explains insistently into a cell phone, as if talking to a toddler.

*I don't know. That's the scary part, I don't know,* yet another whispers as he paces, cigarette in hand, across the cramped width of the sidewalk.

Chances are the schmoozer can take care of himself, but I wonder about the other one; life is hard here for those who confess their fears too freely.

The city has always had almshouses, shadowy repositories for those considered strikingly unsuccessful. In the early years, the impoverished were categorized as *paupers, prostitutes, criminals,* or *mental patients,* and then put into workhouses, if they were potentially productive, or poorhouses, if all such hope had been lost.

Today, we divide ourselves into *haves* and *have-nots,* a more matter-of-fact reckoning that has lately become fashionable. Such stark distinctions are easier to gauge. There are some who have power, wealth, and security, and there are others who simply don't. Even in this rough reckoning, however, the boundaries sometimes blur: those who have more than they ever hoped for never feel that they have quite enough, and some who have very little feel lucky to have that even so.

But nothing is certain in this new world city, save that some of the oldest truths still seem to hold. *Only the little people pay taxes,* one of the haves has told us; *the poor will always be with us,* other experts have explained. Meanwhile, the notion of a widening gap grows ever more pervasive, and frightens even the stoutest members of the vanishing middle class.

*You're going to put me in the poorhouse,* the especially anxious proclaim. It is the age-old dread come back to haunt us, the darker aspect of all that we desire.

Lately, it seems as if much of the city is up for sale. Those who hope for some return on their investment display unwanted possessions on stoops (*Tag sale—misc. treasures & chatchkas*). Though shown to its best advantage, most of the merchandise seems forlorn, as if it has always been old.

Some have decided to leave (*Moving Sale—our loss, your gain*) and offer as expiation an assortment of lamps, end tables, small appliances, and clothes, *all in excellent condition.*

On the corporate level, leases trade hands in accelerated cycles (*EVERYTHING MUST GO!*), though some seem caught in a lingering last-chance limbo. Others have found a more secure market to tap—*We Export to the West Indies*—and do a modest but steady business.

Of course, these are the small companies, the rustic ones still built of bricks and mortar, the visible spectrum of the urban economy. As a general rule, the truly powerful concerns can't be seen by the unaided eye.

Meanwhile, on a downtown street, commerce is incarnated in a young Russian immigrant who hawks posters of Lenin, $20, translation free of charge (*Power to Soviets, Peace to People, Land to Peasants, Factories to Workers*). He does a brisk business; even the buttons from now-ancient military uniforms have been successfully recast as *chatchkas.*

Another vendor chants softly in the heat as he makes a desultory attempt to catch the eye of those who briskly pass by. His lilting island voice can hardly be heard above the traffic.

Years ago, the cries of street peddlers were banned, but today so much noise wells up from the city itself that no one would bother to suppress a single errant song.

Meanwhile, on side streets, the insinuating tune of an ice-cream truck plays on and on and on.

And so the market sings of itself to anyone who will listen.

We have a new term for time: 24/7.

*I'm working like a maniac right now,* a professional woman declares to a friend who nods, knowingly, their paths having crossed during a rash of weekend errands. The speaker seems almost boastful as she rushes about; it might be said that frenzy suits her.

A man on the run expounds his philosophy to an acolyte: *Winning's a habit, just like losing's a habit.* The younger man, craning his head to hear, lags two full steps behind.

But there are those for whom old habits die hard, like the fellow who peddles a paper in the subway—*I AM working, this IS a job*—as he plays to a crowd of unresponsive commuters. He hasn't varied his pitch in years, and no one pays him much attention.

Another underground performer squeezes the life out of a love song, a tattered sign held up for all to see (*My mother has multiple sclerosis and I am blind in one eye*). I'm more familiar with his rendition of the pop tune than I am with the original. Lately, though, he seems to be rushing the song, as if some deadline were looming, as if he, too, were working like a maniac.

It wasn't always that way. On a hot day in the 1940s, during the kind of week where one sees the word *sizzles* over and over in newspaper headlines, almost half the city went to the beach—three million people in shorts and bathing suits declaring a holiday from daily life.

No one would dare to take such liberties now.

It used to be that strangers would declare *Thank God It's Friday* on streets and in bars, but I haven't heard that communal benediction in quite a while. Life in this twenty-first century city has been proclaimed a meritocracy, and no one seems to relax much anymore.

Even those who have time on their hands don't feel easy about it.

*This ain't no fuckin' movie,* a woman shouts into the air one morning as she walks up and down a subway platform. No one pays her much attention. Minutes later, in midtown, a well-known Hollywood star waits for a light as he stands at a corner on Sixth Avenue; at the same moment, a young kid not fifty feet away attempts to ride off with a bike he's just cut free of its lock. But something goes wrong—the bike's owner rushes out of the coffeeshop, wiping his hands on his shirt, screaming at the kid who thought he might escape unobserved but who knows better now, as all eyes turn toward his thin, trembling body and he begins to let go of the bike.

The star, huddled into himself, is the only one who isn't watching the spectacle as it unfolds.

Both celebrity and would-be criminal, it seems, wish to disappear. *This ain't no fuckin' movie.* But the street is no place for the shy. The rest of us, who now constitute a crowd, are free of inhibitions and expect to be entertained.

✦　　　✦　　　✦

The city as movie set: I happen upon one such scene, in a celebrated train terminal, while just passing through one day. A few dozen actor/commuters stand on their marks, in midstride, waiting for the director to call *Action!* Then briefcases and overcoats swing in effortless synchronicity.

They perform this banal sequence repeatedly while those of us in the crowd watch, as if enraptured. It's quite a sight, no doubt, city rubes gawking at faux sophisticates.

I stumble upon another shoot in a downtown neighborhood while on an otherwise unmemorable errand. Most of the passersby have been herded behind barriers and are to be held until the camera stops rolling, but I am allowed, magisterially, to move on through.

*Keep walking and don't look into the camera,* an attendant in headset hisses.

I keep walking. I've been studying for this all my life.

What kind of story have I become part of? I may wonder, in idle moments, but I will likely never know.


Fact: the city is so vast that it dwarfs local disturbances. Neighborhoods can be convulsed and yet the city itself remains calm, unconcerned. It must be frustrating for those trying to get someone's attention, like the forty thousand construction workers, greatly aggrieved, who shut down several square miles of midtown one afternoon. Plasterers, electricians, and pipefitters, all waving signs and shouting.

It must have been something to see.

Of course, most of us didn't see it.


On another occasion a bomb exploded in one of the most recognizable buildings in the world. Those responsible had tried to topple the structure, but apparently little had proceeded according to plan.

I only learned of the incident that evening when I looked out my window and realized that the building itself was missing, its usual place in the skyline nothing but inky darkness.

I was disoriented enough to turn on the television for news. I learned then that the rest of the world already knew all about it.

Throughout the night I watched helicopters, lights pulsing, circle the blinded building like birds of prey. They'd already missed most of the excitement, but weren't about to let anything else slip by them.

Soon enough, it was back to regular programming for the rest of us.


On certain days it seems as if this aging city is crumbling all around us. Bits of bridge buckle, underground pipes, long buried, crack and burst, the streets turn into wild, unnavigable rivers; facades of buildings fall away, so that chunks of brick splatter onto those below like drops of red, muddy rain; fires flare up and smoke darkens the sky.

The cautious walk the streets with care, knowing that the apocalypse, these days, comes in many guises.

Even the experts seem to concur. *Who knows what's going to happen?* a highly placed FBI official remarks, for the record. *It would be foolish for us not to prepare.*

But we have always prepared. After the last great war had ended, and peace seemed at hand, the vigilant began to look ahead to the next conflagration. Plans were made to convert buses into ambulances, children were taught to dive under desks, dehydrated foodstuffs and candles were stockpiled in shelters. But over time, even the anxious wearied of such rehearsals and began, inevitably, to relax. Eventually, someone suggested that the city sell off its air raid sirens.

But recent analyses have indicated that the city is woefully unprepared for even the mildest of modern catastrophes. Microbes and other invisible agents of doom pose the new threat, we are told, more lethal than we can imagine. *The spores of anthrax can live for centuries,* our newspaper informs us. Mock attacks and defense drills are once again in fashion, and volunteer actors agree to collapse on cue so that emergency workers, costumed in cumbersome white survival suits, can pick them up on stretchers and carry them off to shelters.

And officials in neighboring localities have made plans to block off their borders so that the city will be sealed and left to itself, should the worst occur, whatever the worst should prove to be.

Meanwhile, during the most recent crisis, one could for months monitor the *Millennium Clock*: a large billboard-sized display that counted down the days, hours, minutes, and seconds to the advent of the year 2000.

Our computers weren't programmed to handle the sudden onrush of zeros, the experts told us, no one thought ahead years ago when the future seemed still so far away.

But soon enough, they warned, everything that depends upon computers would simply shut down; the electrical grids would fail, the banking system would collapse. No traffic lights, no gas pumps, no ATMs, no cash registers. Chaos would envelop us.

And planes would fall from the sky, some of them surely landing on the city.

✦    ✦    ✦

Each of us was encouraged to put aside stores: three hundred pounds of grain, sixty pounds of sugar, five pounds of salt, twenty pounds of fat or oil for the first year. And keep hard copies of all business records. And learn to use hand tools.

Meanwhile, while waiting, I would wonder: will it be a long, graceful glide through the air or will the planes drop, like a rock, straight down? In stores that autumn, one could buy a book of transcripts from the flight data recorders found at the site of several recent crashes. A number of the terse exchanges ended in a colloquialism that most of us have uttered at some time ourselves:

*Shit.*

Maybe that's all we need to know, and maybe we've always known it.

Though I have seen rock-sized hailstones pelt the streets in late spring, and traces of toxic materials rise up from the bubbling asphalt in the steaming summer, it isn't weather that I worry about. We seem to be safe from the tornadoes, earthquakes, and tsunamis that threaten other places. We will not become Pompeii, or lost Atlantis, or one of those infamous towns leveled by the wayward hand of an angry deity.

Even if intercontinental missiles from hostile powers are aimed directly at us, and we obligingly offer world-class terrorists an easy target, we will probably fall, in the end, from within, on that day when all the worn buildings and bridges and tunnels collapse together, in one last paroxysm of ruin. Only then will the aging city be allowed to rest.

Who else has been lost?

The laborer buried in concrete at a construction site, his

absence noted only after work has broken off for the day, his shaken coworkers left to relive each moment of the shift in their minds. The authorities declare the site a crime scene, just in case.

The judge who jumped into a cab after dinner in midtown decades ago and was never seen again.

And, possibly, the female aviator who hoped to land on a tiny island in the South Pacific but veered off course and just may have ended up here. Why not? *One ocean led naturally to another,* she once wrote about her early travels, and it would not be so fanciful to think that she might have acted on impulse once again. The city, after all, seems always to have attracted the adventurous.

Of course, this is sheer speculation.

One day, no doubt, someone will find the wreckage, the slivers of aluminum coiled around the remains of the antique radio, or the bits of leather jacket pinned down by bone. It's only been sixty years or so, after all, not as long as the average lifetime, and we have the tools now to detect even the most elusive traces of ambition.

If the plane is in the South Pacific, its discovery may take a very long while. But if the plane is somewhere in the city, sooner or later someone is bound to find it.

It's difficult for anything to remain hidden here forever.

Among the city's notable innovations: the country's first roller coaster and its first artificial respirator. One could be forgiven for imagining that the two devices had been designed by the same person.

Wouldn't the same kind of mind conceive of poison and antidote, shock and sedation?

Those who have lived here long enough are used to the swings. It might even be said that only the extremes register, that nothing in the more even middle can command much attention.

The city invention I cherish the most, however, is the simple Yule Log, a crackling simulation of holiday warmth that apartment dwellers could experience just by turning on the television.

It was conceived in the 1950s and was wildly popular from the outset. People would watch the orange glow for hours and fantasize a suburban fireplace.

But times change.

Amusement parks have become dangerous; simulated fright has turned to real as riders, lately, have been thrown from coasters across the country with unsettling regularity.

And last year someone took the Yule Log off the air. That kind of shock might be dangerous as well, in ways we cannot yet fathom.

I sometimes walk past the place where the country's first world's fair was held, over a hundred years ago.

You wouldn't know it now, but someone erected an iron and glass structure here that was hailed as the essence of modernity, the building of the future. And from all accounts it was astonishing: elegant, delicate, flooded with light. People took to calling it a Crystal Palace.

Who would have thought it would burn to the ground in a mere fifteen minutes?

And is it coincidence that the city's first amusement park also burned down, while a million people watched?

*But that's what happens to wood*, some might say. *Aren't glass and metal supposed to be stronger?*

Well, all we can say for sure is that the future isn't fireproof. And maybe it won't be much fun.

Still, in our dreams we design the city of the next millennium, with sleek glass and steel towers that rise like needles into the air. At this very moment, visionaries in five countries around the globe are racing to construct the world's tallest building. Our city of the here-and-now is littered with structures that once claimed that crown, each supplanted by something taller, each reclaimed, in turn, by the entangling hold of the terrestrial.

Meanwhile, in parts of the city today one can find all sorts of short, squat buildings gutted, their blackened windows looking out onto the street like dark empty eyes.

They never had a chance at the title, and they have always known it.

Halfway around the world, in a tiny country that has recently undergone a revolution, the ruling authorities have set out to smash the country's televisions—not those secreted in caves or villages but the thousands of sets hidden away in the cities.

The crusaders aim to *kill urban communication,* a Western expert states.

Well, it would never work here.

Say you could confiscate the televisions, radios, cell phones, computers, and CB sets that abound in the city; shut down the networks and cable channels; board up the subways, airports, and bus stations; and close off the streets.

Say you could force people to stay away from their windows, so that no one could speak to or signal anyone else, and then separate members of families or households, even at that your work would have just begun.

People will always talk, if only to themselves.

Even if you could reduce the sound of the city to a single voice, it would still be a veritable Tower of Babel.

But even conventional communication isn't always necessary.

This is, after all, the place to which the most famous deaf, dumb, and blind woman of her time would rush when she felt a little lonely. She sometimes thought of herself as a shadow, moving about in a dream, but she knew that on her trips to the city she would awaken again to the world.

It was a kind of resurrection.

She especially liked riding the subway. No need to dream there, not in a place where eighteen hundred people can spill out of a single train in less than sixty seconds. No need for speech or sight, such partial capacities, in that circumstance; one needs only a willingness to merge into a single being, more than merely human.

She was a natural. She became, in a sense, the quintessential city person.

Sometimes, I attempt to practice random acts of awareness, if only to dispel, for a time, my abiding sense of unknowing.

But just as often I miss things.

If I had been alert one day not long ago, I might have taken notice of the thief who pilfered 14,000 quarters collected from the 65,000 parking meters that line the city streets. He was caught with 295 of those quarters in his pockets. They must have weighed him down, made it difficult to walk; an observant witness surely would have noticed his labored shuffle or heard the loud jangling that marked his every movement.

But no one, it seems, saw or heard anything at all.

The fellow was caught, finally, by a surveillance camera in a grocery store. I'd been in another part of the city altogether, watching something else, like the slow-witted mark on the street who never sees the pea as it's switched from shell to shell.

Some time before that, the Dow fell 512 points in one day, the dollar thirteen percent in one week. Much of the city went into mourning for the market. I hadn't seen that one coming either, though financial convulsions are increasingly common, and currencies—the yen, the deutsche mark, the ruble, the dollar—are said to plunge, slide, and crash as if almost animate. Some follow the ups and downs of these elements as if they were auguries.

Others are not certain they really want to know.

Fact: *Customer Shoots 3 in Crowded Restaurant,* the newspaper announces one day. One minute cocktail conversation, idle fiddling with swizzle sticks, plates of bread or salad passed around; the next minute loud pops, screams, the sharp tinkle of shattered china. Liquids seep from glasses and cups, while ice cubes spin in manic fashion across the floor.

Those customers who are unharmed hardly dare to move, as if trying to stay with a story that's been interrupted, ever so rudely, in midsentence.

There's no way to prepare for surprise, per se. It's not as if one could know ahead of time (*why fuss about what to order? I won't be able to finish it*). But once the unlikely has occurred, it seems inevitable, as if the whole of one's day has been heading straight for that one moment.

It's nature's way of sustaining the narrative.

Fact: Six thousand bolts of lightning per minute strike somewhere on the planet's surface. One day, one of them happened to land near me. I hadn't been on water, or under a tree, or in any of the usual places, but the bolt sought me out even so, 1.5 million volts of electricity, more or less, directed at a little room on the top floor of a building indistinguishable from all the others on the block.

It was hard to avoid a sense of being singled out.

One minute silence, the next the loudest crack I have ever heard, the kind of sound conveyed in the large cartoonish letters that spell out *WHAM!* or *ZAP!* in comic books. Then a bluish glow that sizzled along the baseboards.

For a moment I thought about calling someone, but the phone line had been knocked out.

I went down to the street. A few others were looking up at the place where the bolt had struck just above my window. I looked up too. There wasn't much to say.

Much later, I came across a headline in the paper: *When Lightning Strikes, Lives are Changed.*

But how, I wonder. How?

One night, on my way home, I happen upon something that has just begun to burn in the middle of the street. It flares up like a bonfire, there's something beautiful about it, the yellow-orange spikes of flame piercing the midnight sky. *What is it,* I wonder. A stranger who's come out of his apartment in his pajamas approaches me.

*What is it?* he asks, as if I have the answer.

I peer more intently at the fireball. Anything made of fabric or flesh has already been burnt away, but I think I can see, through the flames, the metallic outline of what could once have been a windshield.

*Maybe it's a car.*

If so, it's impossible to tell whether anyone is in it.

The fire trucks arrive. Once the water hits the flames we're driven back by noxious clouds of smoke. After a few minutes the bystanders begin to drift away, as does the smoke itself. Even the firefighters are ready to move on. I'm the only one left who's still looking at the now-sodden lump of something.

The next day I return to the scene. Nothing's left of the night before except a dark stain on the street and a blackened bit of rubber. The carcass itself has long since been hauled away. In another day or so, a good spring rain will wash the street clean.

Just weeks later, a neighbor two doors down is killed in a mid-day fire that takes seven fire trucks to extinguish.

She had lived on the top floor too. Her apartment was probably laid out very much like mine. But I didn't know her. I can't even say for sure whether I ever saw her.

I hadn't been in the neighborhood that day. When I came home that evening, I couldn't see the dark smudges on brick or the broken windows. There was no sign on the street that anything untoward had happened.

But the next day I heard the story and went out to look for myself.

Large sheets of plastic had been hung across the window frames, flapping in the breeze, softly, making no sound. What was left of the shutters, scraps of wood, really, were hanging at a careless angle where a fireman's axe had struck them. There was nothing but darkness inside, walls and wood charred black.

A multicolored child's drawing hung undisturbed on the window of the apartment below.

It was quiet on the street. A few onlookers were weaving the story into a kind of impromptu ode.

*She was young*
*she was 40*
*she was drinking*
*she was smoking*
*she passed out*
*it's all gone*
*the apartment was gutted.*

Her dog had been carried to safety when the fire broke out and had begun to run in wild circles around the stoop. People thought he was playing. By the time he ran back into the building, it was too late to bring him out again.

So we lost two neighbors, really.

That week my landlady inspects my apartment, searching for anything that can be considered combustible. She glances about and waves her hands extravagantly, trying to bridge the language barrier. But I can't understand her. She switches to English and points.

*Books, books, fire, fire . . .*

She laments in this truncated way for a long while, then leaves.

Now I worry too. The bright red extinguisher I hung years ago in the kitchen is coated with dust and seems very small all of a sudden, as if a little plastic fireman's hat ought to have come with it. Even if I wasn't drunk, didn't nod off, hadn't passed out, how could I ever contain the flames once the books began to smolder?

Philosophy would go first, then fiction, adventure, finance, all those flimsy paperbacks. Finally the dusty Bible itself would ignite, its tissue-thin pages curling as they fed the fire.

And everything I had thought worth pondering upon would go up, as they say, in smoke.

The greatest library of the ancient world, in its day, contained over five hundred thousand delicate papyrus scrolls, state-of-the-art scholarship, collected and exhibited in the world's most vibrant city. That library was incinerated in some kind of conflagration. In its aftermath, the accumulated thought of the ages vanished from the earth for over a thousand years.

For every ancient text that was eventually reconstituted, they say, forty-some other works were lost forever.

And the imposing city that housed the library is now little more than a backwater, overshadowed for millennia by newer, more energetic urban upstarts.

The diligent humanists who created the monumental *Encyclopédie* in the eighteenth century believed that the volumes they were compiling in such painstaking manner would preserve, in definitive fashion, all that was worth knowing. If something were ever to happen, if a catastrophe of unthinkable proportions should wipe out the civilized world, knowledge could be summoned again (they presumed) by consulting these books, with their detailed diagrams, explanations, and drawings.

Indeed, the *Encyclopédie* has survived, though no one cares much about tanneries or blacksmithing today.

I wouldn't think to compare my tiny repository to the more august institutions of its kind that abound. And it wouldn't be much of a loss anyway, should my own collection burn: one's books are more of a burden, those unread an open rebuke, it might almost be a relief if suddenly, through some unknown agency, they were all to disappear.

But how I would miss the newspaper clippings!

I thought about the woman and the fire whenever I walked past her apartment for the next few days, over a long holiday weekend. The place that had been hers and would shortly be rented out to someone else. A demolition company had already hung its sign out front, trolling for future business.

I thought about her one afternoon that week as I was walking in a different part of the city, my reverie abruptly interrupted by a mechanical screech and then a loud, extended thud. A couple near me pointed up the block in disbelief. They were looking at a cab that had come to a dead stop in the middle of the street.

*He hit one,* the man gasped.

*He hit two,* the woman retorted, as if correcting the record.

I turned to look too. I wasn't thinking about the woman anymore; the city itself had changed the subject.

What else vanishes? What other parts of ourselves slowly begin to slip away?

I sometimes think of that lone castaway, left in that remote place, who kept a meticulous account of his doings every day for years, each concretely rendered experience contributing, bit by bit, to the lasting impression of a life.

He possessed more than enough paper. But one day, in a dark reckoning, he realized that he would eventually run out of ink.

There were no ships on the horizon poised to send in fresh supplies. Only one course, it seems, was left to him—a ruthless winnowing of the remarkable from the ordinary, the less vivid events left to fade as memory failed, until the last few drops of the black fluid had been drained and his bold script reduced to faint scratches.

After that: unthinking immersion in the here-and-now, a kind of drowning in the present moment.

But we don't drown easily. We flail away at the future, we struggle to hold on to the past.

It would be so much simpler if we could just make our peace with the blank page.

I have learned that the word for *city* is the same as the word for *wall* in at least one ancient language. It's a clever idea, actually, designing the notion of defense into the very conception of the city itself.

But whatever shuts some out at the same time shuts others in.

External foes, internal tensions, the city contorted, like a Möbius strip, as it tries to watch over all aspects of itself simultaneously.

The old walls, most of stone, were sometimes sixty feet thick. The modern city requires something lighter, more imaginative, almost metaphorical.

An early sociologist spoke of the *blasé attitude,* a kind of blankness that the savvy city dweller adopts, like a mask, to guard against the intrusions of strangers. It's the closest thing to invisibility that modernity can devise.

And, it seems, a most successful adaptation. What's *mask,* after all, but another word for *wall?*

But it took a visionary to show us how one could hide behind a smile even more effectively than a blank expression. He perfected the genial facade, the armored shield of affability.

He also engineered the first national theme park and has since shaped much of the world's imagination. But he was always something of an urban planner at heart, a utopian, who fell into the business of amusement while hungering to conceive the City of Tomorrow.

His first such effort was a 160-acre enclave designed expressly *to keep the outside world from intruding upon you.* He named it after himself, and directed that its grubby infrastructure be hidden, so that visitors could wolf down hot dogs and colas and toss aside trash that magically disappeared. There were rides and exhibits, as one would expect, but the real attraction lay in experiencing the unremittingly pleasant nature of the place. Nothing quite like it existed anywhere else.

He built an apartment above its central street so that he might watch over his works like a deity, ever alert, easily displeased.

If he had to, he would force people to have fun.

I played with a popular scale model of that magical place on my living room rug when I was a child, moving tiny vehicles and green plastic shrubbery around, propelling the cartoon characters and little people from one exotic quadrant to another. I imagined resistance when I put them back in the box; it seemed to me that they didn't want to leave the sixteen square feet of utopia any more than I did.

Over time, the shabby outside world closed in on the master's first creation, suffocating it with strip malls and the tacky detritus of urban life, until even he turned away.

He started over again, on the other side of the country, vowing to create *a whole new shiny city* from scratch. It was to be a community free of discord, unemployment, slums, all the societal ills that were consuming real cities. Every street would be a Main Street, buffed to an eye-straining shine.

It was to be the kind of place where problems could be whisked away. Who would need the police, for instance, when citizens could use rounds of *paper, scissors, rock* to resolve any conflicts that arose?

But it was never meant to be perfect. It would be a *community of tomorrow that will never be completed,* the future by definition unfinished.

He died before his gleaming city could be constructed, and the dream too seemed to die without its dreamer.

Lately, however, the corporate entity has returned to its utopian roots. A pristine community has arisen under its aegis, an old-fashioned city/town that life-sized people live in. It's become an attraction in its own right, as well as a movie set upon occasion. Visitors find its nostalgic facades and tidy front porches fascinating.

Some think the place intolerably unnatural, but others are drawn to the idea of a city without shadows, a city, as it were, that always smiles.

It's clearly something that people will pay for.

✦       ✦       ✦

A case study in *cause and effect*: sometimes, city people descend unwittingly into the subway only to discover that the trains aren't running, service interrupted *due to an earlier incident*. That's all they ever tell us, whoever they are; we're left, as we wait, to piece together the likeliest scenarios ourselves.

There isn't much else to do, once the news has subsided and the last person has hissed her *not again* in a soft undertone of complaint.

The dictionary defines *incident* as *a seemingly minor occurrence that can lead to serious consequences*. Something containable spirals out of control, like the butterfly's flutter in South America that prompts hurricane-force winds to whip the coast a thousand miles away.

It's relatively easy to imagine city analogues.

Was the mildly disagreeable mood of one person inadvertently passed on to another, building in intensity, until whole trains were infused with a foul feeling and the system itself ground to a stop?

Or did a stray look mutate into a stare, ad infinitum, so that eventually everyone underground was plunged into a paralytic state of self-consciousness?

Experts who have devoted a lifetime to the study of complex man-made systems now propose a new category of experience: the *normal accident*. In such thinking, it is assumed routinely that unexpected incidents will occur, accidents will happen, chaos will always be with us. Our task, as realists, is to accept the inexplicable, since it's likely to erupt, sooner or later, whether we wish it or not, especially if we find ourselves in a city.

So say the experts. But most of us, inveterate amateurs, can't disengage from the need for narrative.

We still want to know *why*.

Occasionally, I foresee something that has already happened, tapping into the kind of psychic power available to all but rarely claimed.

One week, I had fallen behind in my reading and went through the newspapers several days late. One article seemed especially provocative: *Ailing 6-Year-Old Disappears, and Police Seek His Sitter*. Awful, of course, but the kind of thing that happens every day in a city as large as this one.

But I knew from television reports that the young boy had already been returned to his family, unharmed, and that the sitter had been detained to await the expected psychiatric evaluation. I knew that her neighbors had recovered from the initial shock of the news, had already shaken their heads, shrugged, and turned again to their own troubles. I knew that the reporters had gone on to another story, another dim narrative taking shape in half-intelligible fashion before them.

But how odd to return to that moment when the mystery is still fresh, when nothing is known for sure, when there are just a series of dark possibilities to ponder. *Maybe we're going to hear something,* the boy's father hopes, proving that he too is a prophet.

Once again the enduring question almost asks itself: how else could the story have ended?

Every so often I pick up bits of stories on the streets, tantalizing in their incompleteness. One woman declares to a companion *I have something to tell you* at the very moment that I pass; but I am rushing onward, fated to miss the moment of revelation. All I know is that the woman is nervous, and her friend seems to stiffen as he waits for her to continue.

*That's a classic symptom of anxiety,* a man announces to a woman. Immediately I watch for signs of instability. She seems more frail now than at first glance.

*It's not how much money you have,* an older woman explains to a younger. If she had more money, I wonder, would she be sitting here on the pavement outside a parking garage?

*I live life one day at a time,* a man of indeterminate age, ragged coat, baseball cap, and backpack observes as he leans into a car window. Is he a garrulous host bidding farewell to his guests, or a drifter who holds forth at red lights?

*Somebody's always getting shot at on Saturday night,* one youth says to another. Why are these young men laughing? Why not?

*I didn't know you were supposed to shout "BINGO,"* a teenager says, tensely, as he rushes alongside three older men. His elders look at each other and nod.

*Before coming here I spent two and a half years in Brazil and nine years in Norway,* a young woman explains to an acquaintance.

At last: a fragment that makes sense. *The roller coaster and respirator.*

And I am able to make a prediction: I don't know about the others, but I believe that this young woman will be happy here.

On one street in the city one brownstone stands apart from the others, like an especially flamboyant member of a crowd. I pass the building almost every day. It was once something of a bomb factory. Now it's noted for the chic architectural refashioning of its lower floors, blasted beyond recognition in the unintended conflagration of 1970. Traces of the three who died here on that day have also been effaced. A survivor, a fugitive who hid for years in the underground before capture, is identified in radical histories as a *North American anti-imperialist*—something of a rare breed these days. She's still locked up.

Down the block, at a school founded by émigrés who were abruptly uprooted themselves, someone is offering a lecture this week: *Hemophilia: Yesterday, Today, Tomorrow.*

But who can foretell the future? No one on this block, it seems, has ever been much good at it.

Fact: the land the city rests upon was purchased for $24 in the old days, the city founded on what many consider a cold-hearted act of commerce.

There have been many such acts since.

Unfortunates in eighteenth century jails were sometimes imprisoned for debts of less than $10. Today, it costs the city $54 to buy the wooden boxes that descendants of these pioneering indigents are buried in.

One afternoon, as I'm walking to the post office, I see a guard outside a bank nervously finger a gun he's taken out of its holster. An armored car idles nearby, its thick doors open. The man swings his arm in slow agitation, the sheen of the 9mm catching what can still be seen of the sun in the overcast sky. Meanwhile, a toddler with parent in tow lurches out of a nearby McDonald's. He's clutching something too, a lone french fry that he's holding aloft, studying the salty golden strip as if it too were a treasure.

Something could happen here, in this moment, if the guard got spooked, or the boy began to run toward the truck, or someone in the shadows suddenly stepped out and moved toward the money.

Maybe the gun would go off, and someone would scream, while others melted into doorways and disappeared.

At the very least the little boy might drop his food and start to wail.

But, as it happens, nothing special is to occur on this corner on this day.

I never do see the money. I only see the gun.

In 1896, some 150,000 city shoppers attended the festive unveiling of the newly dubbed *department store*. Its resplendent goods, piled in stacks one could set a straight edge to, glittered behind windows of plate glass, the whole illuminated by the splendor of electric light.

Indeed, an early utopian tract conceived of the world as a shopping mall.

Today, one vestige of this pure vision remains, an oasis of commerce, in a chic section of the city. It's become the most expensive retail district per square foot in the world. Along this strip the merchandise is costly enough to be hung, casually, on bare metal racks and shelves that gleam, behind windows so polished they seem to be on sale themselves.

It's as if only the idea of exchange is on display. Indeed, money in its more tangible forms would seem untoward here. One can hardly imagine a clerk in these boutiques touching the stained bills or dirty coins that most of us keep, without thinking, in our pockets.

I don't shop in this district myself. But I do spend much of my money in the city. Last year, according to the city's own calculations, I paid $5.15 for libraries, $35.78 for jails. And another 57¢ for snow removal.

I got the snow for free.

One night I find myself watching the first few minutes of the sequel to a famous horror film being shown again on television. In this opening scene two children, still in their pajamas, are sent up the street by their babysitter to get help. It's dark; the setting would spook most city people even if there weren't a maniac at large. Too much open space, too many trees, cars parked aimlessly, as if waiting for something, anything, to happen. The kids have been told to knock on doors, wake the neighbors, call the police, get through at any cost before the killer regains consciousness.

It's a two-minute reprise of the original, enough to remind us that there's no place more dangerous than a quiet, empty street, a threat of which only the foolishly myopic characters in a movie would be unaware.

The film is supposed to take place in the Midwest. But this sequence was actually shot in a suburb outside the city, in the childhood home of someone I know. He was only a toddler when his parents rented out the house. I wonder what it must have been like to walk up those stairs, into that room, keep your clothes in that closet, look out that window at night.

He swears it didn't affect him, but even make-believe horror must have lingering repercussions.

Unless we know better than to be scared by anything anymore.

✦    ✦    ✦

I have studied another haunted house, in another city, at much closer range. It was the scene of a notorious double murder whose grisly specifics mesmerized much of the country.

I was visiting someone a few years after the incident and we drove up the street on a whim, late at night, looking for the infamous two-story condo. I joked about finding the still-missing murder weapon. The shock of the event had long since been stripped away, the story played out in an infinite media loop, but surely the real place would possess some residual power, some element of the experience that couldn't be conveyed at a distance.

It was a pilgrimage, if you will, to a spot where the mythic accretion of urban dread was still at an early stage.

We had to be within yards of the place itself, but nothing looked familiar. I walked back and forth along the short block. The street was poorly lit, but even in the midnight haze it looked utterly ordinary. Nothing, really, like those menacing streets in the movies that make even a jaded viewer shiver.

How could anything horrific possibly have happened here?

I crossed the street to get one last look at the spot from farther back.

Abruptly I felt a shock of recognition, as if the film had finally come into focus. The trees and the windows I now saw above the wall were more familiar than those outside my own apartment; they'd served as the backdrop for hundreds of television remotes. The architectural details of the space outside the entranceway had been reconfigured, the wall itself redesigned, so that it was possible, even likely, that one could pass the altered area without realizing it.

But now the demystifying spell had been broken.

Indeed, it was difficult to conceive that this could ever have been a place where ordinary people lived, that someone had been eating ice cream inside in the minutes before opening that door for the last time. Now it was dark, and forbidding, like a castle seen in the distance from an empty Transylvanian road.

With just a hint of sadness, as if a trace of something real still remained.

If this were a movie, I thought, I wouldn't want to see the sequel.

Here's another city story, almost canonical, a rumination upon the age-old theme of *wrong place, wrong time,* fate determined by accident rather than design.

It's three A.M., one weekend night in the sixties, time to close up the bar you manage and head home. You're in your mid-twenties, the kind of girl who can have your picture taken alongside dozens of liquor bottles and still look like an innocent.

You probably think there's nothing special about this night, the one that's all but over. You're probably looking forward to Sunday morning.

But somebody sees you as you lock the door and drive off, someone who's been cruising the streets looking for a girl just like you. He makes a sudden U-turn and trails you intently for miles.

You probably haven't noticed him yet, though we will never know for certain.

We do know that you see him after you've parked, and begin to run, and almost reach your front door.

And we know that the moments that follow will make you famous.

✦    ✦    ✦

But you'll have to share that attention with others. Because what happened to you that night will always be overshadowed by the actions that didn't occur. By the thirty-eight neighbors who didn't call the police, or open their windows or doors, though all of them could see you on the ground. (Everybody, it seems, was watching you that night.) Studies will be done in the future about these folks, and mention of your name will always evoke thoughts of them.

It's nothing personal. It's just that your one life has been emptied into the larger being of the city itself.

It's probably little consolation, but for your sacrifice you're sure to live forever in the mythic annals of metropolitan life.

Not everyone in the city is bent on murder. Some folks just want to have fun.

Every few years or so, it seems, someone leaps from the city's tallest structures, in free fall 110 or 86 stories above the streets until the moment the parachute opens. Most land safely, but the risk of catastrophe is real. *You never know what you're going to land on,* one thrill-seeker acknowledges. A few unfortunates have been entangled in traffic lights and left to dangle until arrested, but those who can pack up their equipment quickly enough vanish into the normal rush and tumble of city traffic, never to be identified.

It must be disappointing to have to run and hide after renouncing anonymity so dramatically. Almost daring people to watch. And watch they will: fingers pointed upward, eyes shielded from the sun, mesmerized, following the graceful descent of the chute for the full minute or two it takes to hit the ground.

I happened to be gazing at that landmark building from my window, as I sometimes do, on the very day two young men leapt off. I was miles away, but I could see flash bulbs popping on the observation deck as dusk began to fall, the tiny explosions coming in clusters, like flack in an old war film. For me that was show enough and I turned away.

Minutes later the jumps occurred.

Like many in the city, I wish I'd seen the spectacle. Now, I can only imagine the two chutes swaying and drifting for the few seconds I would have seen them.

The authorities discourage such daredeviltry. *It's a stupid and jerky thing to do,* the mayor himself has observed. Police officers have been instructed to isolate anyone who threatens to jump from the city's taller structures.

But it's hopeless, for there will always be those in the city who wish to fly, or to fall, to resist the crush of the concrete world around them.

More city sport: one man sprints after another down the middle of a narrow street in late afternoon on a crisp fall day. His quarry pulls ahead, almost effortlessly, leaving the out-of-shape fellow to fall ever farther behind.

*Fucking faggot! Slow down!* the leaden fellow shouts.

The faster one, who has spurted ahead, looks back once before confidently disappearing into traffic. The slower one stumbles, holding his heaving chest, as if the very effort to shape the epithet has exhausted him.

*When you have something hidden in your heart, it's going to keep coming to the surface.*

So speaks a woman whose husband has just confessed to a

crime, an act he kept hidden for almost twenty years. With the aid of a pastor he has confronted himself, and taken a long look at the dark thing he did to someone else, in another lifetime, so very long ago.

It didn't happen here. But the juxtaposition of crime and contrition, what we have come to call *closure,* was striking enough to have found its way to the national section of our newspaper.

What's hidden, one wonders, in the heart of the city?

Crime, of course—crime and malice, cops and robbers, cases that haven't been closed, the stuff of the tabloid imagination. In 1903 a body was found hidden in a barrel here, and for a time the entire city recoiled at its disturbing disposition. The crime, though never solved, was finally attributed to a criminal underclass that only harms its own. So most of the city seemed to be safe.

Just last month, another body in a barrel was discovered in the city. It was tucked into the crawl space under a modest home here. On the surface, everything tidy and unsurprising; nothing but disorder underneath.

So far, we know only that the latest victim was a woman. And that she wore a ring inscribed with the phrase *Love Uncle Phil.*


But there is something else hidden in the heart of the city, something simmering just below the surface. It might come upon us suddenly (*an ice cart, a barrel, a bomb*) or might creep up ever so slowly, taking years to find its shape, until the image we see of a stranger in the mirror or the window takes us sharply by surprise.

We can dodge and weave and run but it waits for us, this

reckoning, which some call *fate* or *destiny,* others the *last chapter* or *third act*.

Like many in the city, this is one tale I'm not eager to see to the end.

*Feeling weak? A little bit under the weather? Maybe you ought to lie down. You probably have some questions. It never hurts to ask, but it may sting some when you don't get any answers.*

*You want to know: when did the fever start? At what point will it break?*

*Is it when you realize you can't stay out of the streets, but can't leave your room, can't stay awake, but can't fall asleep, can't live with it, can't live without it, even if you're not sure, after all these years, just what "it" really is?*

*Welcome to the city, the place where all contrary indications hold true.*

*Beginning to feel better?*

It's been a year since anyone occupied the apartment on the top floor of the little building tucked into a small street in the financial district. Its windows are empty, pools of darkness in an area that is beginning to brighten as the neon sheen of night arises.

The building itself seems out of place, a cozy enclave dwarfed by more imposing structures.

Certainly it's an unlikely site for a crime scene or, more precisely, a foul deed that no one can yet prove has happened.

But one day two middle-aged artists left the apartment for a walk and haven't been seen since. Investigators later found passports, wallets, keys, all the usual accoutrements of the usual life left on a kitchen counter.

The only suspect under serious suspicion is the landlord, who disappeared himself for two weeks after the incident occurred. He's back now, tending shop on the ground floor, denying any knowledge of a rent dispute, declaring himself as befuddled as anyone about what happened to his two tenants.

He'd like to sell the building.

No one seems to believe his story—even the police, who must call it a missing persons case, consider it a double homicide—but dark suspicions do not afford tangible evidence of misdoings. In the eyes of the law, the two have simply gone out and—who knows?—might return at any moment.

On this particular night in late fall, friends of the couple have gathered to hold an anniversary vigil for their lost neighbors. The two haven't grown any older in the last year, judging from the picture that is propped up on an easel.

A candle burns on a little table set out on the stoop. Six people shiver in the cold. They talk to anyone who stops, talk about their neighbors, about the mystery, the ache of all those questions.

What's the worst of it? *No body, no crime,* says a woman in her forties. How does it feel to see the prime suspect every day? *I have to live somewhere. And I have a right to my home.*

The candle flickers. Passersby drop donations in a bucket, the funds to be used for xeroxing, postage, and such, the small but steady costs of keeping the quest alive.

One remaining news truck is parked along the street. Later, the local station will air a story that lasts for fifteen seconds.

Someone has offered a private reward. It's been rising over the months and is now at $20,000. The money hasn't yet flushed out any information. No one has confessed, or snitched, or even hinted at an outcome. But the police are sure that somebody somewhere knows something.

Meanwhile, the friends circulate an open letter: *Please help us in the search for answers.*

The message is formally addressed to the mayor, but it's actually being sent to anyone who may still be out there, the weary city talking softly to itself.

One day I notice a sign hung at chest level on a telephone pole. *FOUND GRAY BUNNY,* it proclaims, in a child's careful lettering.

Up the block a few stuffed animals are scattered on the sidewalk. A man walking briskly along the avenue sees them, breaks his stride, and stops.

*There's a bear over there,* he announces, speaking to the woman who's come to a halt beside him.

She's looking at a large mouse that lies in the gutter, at a rakish angle, its pink ears pinned against a car.

The bear is gray, too, but once was white. He's on his back, paws sticking up.

No one seems to be searching for Mr. Bear or Mr. Mouse. But at least one of their companions, I assume, has been safely scooped up from the street.

Fact: it's been many years since the day a thirty-seven-year-old man shot four kids in the subway. He claimed that he fired in self-defense. Others were sure that he was motivated by sheer malevolence. The issue was debated throughout the world.

I took that same train all the time back then, though I wasn't there on that day.

A few years later, I saw the shooter on the street, a thin, edgy figure even slighter than I'd imagined.

He didn't seem much of a threat anymore. Except, perhaps, as a cautionary tale, living proof of the careless disregard for consequences.

How chilling must it be, after all, to have shaped your life in one moment, one act, so that your story is forever bound to words like *before* and *after?*

Sometimes, people try to make sense of the city together, like the two small children, possibly sisters, who find themselves caught in a conundrum while they wait for the subway they've boarded to pull out of the station. The train has surfaced at a stop aboveground but is soon to glide underground again. In the meantime, its passengers sit in limbo, most in a kind of submissive unconcern, as the girls' voices carry through the car.

*We're inside,* the smaller one insists.

*No, we're outside,* the other girl, older, snaps back.

*Inside!*

*Outside!*

And so it goes, with the exaggerated exactitudes of childhood. The older girl's irritation is growing, preternaturally, as if there's a churlish adult incubating inside her. She shakes her head and sighs. The younger girl just sits, lost in thought, pressing her small round face against the window.

Neither one speaks.

The train begins to pull away and slowly sinks into the ground. Still, the little girl peers out, her eyes fixed, though all she can see is darkness.

✦　　✦　　✦

Every day, in the back pages of the paper, the city takes note of those whose lives have slipped away, ever so quietly, as if by stealth. Recently we lost an eighty-five-year-old Cardiologist and Educator, an eighty-one-year-old Pioneer in Film Animation, a seventy-two-year-old Doctor Who Wrote on Eating Disorders, an eighty-seven-year-old Archaeologist, and a number of other people who Didn't Do Much of Anything while alive. These less distinguished departed receive a one-line mention in tiny type; you have to be looking for it in order to find it, as with so much else here, and the odds of the reference remaining unseen are considerable.

But at least that way there's a chance.

If someone neglects even to place your name in the newspaper, as has surely happened, then *poof!*—you simply disappear.

But sometimes, in that moment before the rupture closes over, someone notices the anomaly, as did the twenty-nine-year-old lawyer who tracked down the man she'd seen in her neighborhood park, month after month, until the week he failed to show up and she began to worry. She knew nothing about him except that he walked his German shepherd every day. She didn't know that he lived alone, on disability, and was what the world might consider a lost soul.

When she finally found him, in a room in a cheap neighborhood hotel, his recumbent dog beside him, he had apparently been dead for some days.

She posted a flier around the neighborhood announcing a makeshift memorial service. One cold morning a few other pet owners gathered in the park to mark the man's passing. One of them, a reporter, subsequently declared the deceased a Solitary Man in the human interest piece in the Metro section of our newspaper.

We also learned, in that piece, that the man had named his dog Hamlet.

She may live for years to come, this young lawyer, she may distinguish herself in the corporate world by crafting dazzling multimillion-dollar deals, but in the lasting annals of the city she will be known in simpler fashion, as the person who remembered the forty-two-year-old Fellow Who Was Almost Forgotten.

More city sport: a car jumps the curb and knocks down three people strolling outside a department store; days later, a twenty-three-ton truck crashes into a small shop, sending a parked car perilously close to an onlooker. *I had the Koran in my hand, so I just started praying,* the man remarks afterward, clutching his text even more tightly.

Though the one behind the wheel is usually at fault, the police department maintains a Division of Driverless Cars, just in case.

But even the most thorough preparation cannot account for every possibility.

One day, a woman bustling off to a meeting in midtown is struck by the errant arm of an elderly man who has jumped from the building above her. She crumples to the ground but survives. *You hear stories about debris falling,* she notes, *but you never hear about people falling.* One wonders how long she's lived here. She is speaking now from the safety of a neighboring state.

Meanwhile, there are notices in the subway—*Awake is aware*—that remind us all of the abiding rule of city life.

✦　　✦　　✦

Other fragments of city stories:

• *She kept her mouth shut,* a woman shouts into a pay phone, as if she wants the whole city to hear.

• *I don't understand Chinese but I'm not illiterate,* a young kid on the street spits out. He's been dissed. His companions tease him, mimic him, mock him, but he can't stop worrying the story. The woman he speaks of is first only vaguely sketched as he sputters, but becomes *that fool, that bitch,* in the space of half a block.

Listening to these snippets is like being a tourist, taking the city in one small dose at a time.

Sometimes even the newspaper of record raises more questions than it resolves. *Two Friends Arrested in Unrelated Slayings,* a short article observes, as if that's all there is to it.

But what's the story, I wonder: that friends can kill, or that killers have friends?

Fact: someone has found the body of a climber, undisturbed for seventy-five years, close to the top of the world's tallest mountain. Someone else speculates that the climber may actually have been the first to scale the peak, anticipating by almost thirty years the feat of the man who's made the claim in the history books.

But who can really say?

Those who recovered the body are looking for a camera, for an old roll of undeveloped film that might contain images of the indisputable: a picture taken at the top, an unobstructed view, nothing but clouds, the world laid out in sunken splendor below. Or a fuzzy self-portrait, a man standing stiffly at the summit, his goal achieved, the rest of his life extending emptily before him.

Was he on his way up, or down?

The bones themselves, long since settled into the ice, yield nothing.

That same week, another group locates the remains of a space capsule lost for thirty-eight years. It's on the bottom of the ocean. It was supposed to have been retrieved after its fifteen-minute flight, but something went awry and it sank.

The experts hope, by examining the wreckage, to resolve a mystery that's persisted all these years. Why did the hatch blow off so early? Did the pilot astronaut panic?

He was killed a few years after the flight. He always refused to admit to any wrong.

His widow, meanwhile, has asked that the capsule remain undisturbed. She isn't curious about what happened. Or maybe she's afraid to find out.

But how can she expect us to tolerate the mystery?

She's resisting the very essence of the anxious culture that surrounds her.

One week a visitor sets out to claim a world record, scaling five city bridges in four hours. He's climbed in public before in other places, he's famous for it. He chooses to begin his challenge here with the most celebrated of the group, an elegant but unforgiving structure that claimed its own designer before the last stone was set in place a hundred and some years earlier. This time, it's no contest, the climber loses his footing soon after he starts up and slips downward, his glide impossible to arrest.

No one records the fall itself, but there's a picture in the paper of the empty alleyway where he landed.

That same season, a bad one for keeping one's balance, a salesman dies after plunging thirteen stories through a floor-to-ceiling plate-glass window. He had just signed off on a multi-million-dollar business deal. *The last time we saw him,* someone on the scene noted, *he was laughing.*

No one knows when the laughter stopped.

Some in the city have always been risk-averse, so much so that others, bolder, have had to propel them forward in spite of themselves.

When an intrepid young entrepreneur invented the first passenger elevator, long ago, he tried to sell it in this very city. But early sales were inexplicably slow. The young man made impassioned predictions, assured his skeptical audiences that the city would shoot upward, unimaginably, into the sky, into the future, but the pitch wasn't very persuasive. Some were intrigued, but most people, all those potential passengers, wished simply to stay rooted.

He knew he'd have to show them.

One day, at a citywide exposition, he stepped into his cage, alone, and rode up into the air. Spectators had to crane their necks simply to see him. Once suspended, far above their heads, he issued the command.

*Cut the rope!*

The small platform that had held him aloft began to plunge toward the crowd. Good-hearted people on the ground gasped. But he wasn't screaming or even making a sound as he fell. He knew that his fortune, his future, was safe.

Sure enough, the mechanism broke his fall. Sales of the

new contraption soon skyrocketed. Even the most reluctant were now enticed into the air, and the city began its dramatic vertical ascent.

Some claim now that our ancient apprehensions are outmoded, that cities today extend horizontally rather than upward, that height itself is nothing to be feared any longer.

But I've been to those horizontal cities, and I wonder: isn't zooming along a freeway simply falling sideways?

*So where does the story take place?*

*One possibility: the story takes place in the city. But what city? Surely not just the one I happen to live in. No, the city is growing, spreading, testing its limits like a newly emboldened force of nature.*

*It's one thing to pore over reports of such mutation; it's more startling to see the shift depicted viscerally in drawings, the kind of visual aids that alarmists have devised to shock us into awareness.*

*They worry that images are all we can really read anymore.*

*The maps compiled by these anxious experts show the cities of the world as red circles, some large, like open wounds, others just pinpricks, hardly drawing blood. That, they tell us, is bound to change.*

*In time, just one world city will form, thousands of red circles seeping into one another. Our once-blue planet will turn crimson.*

*That won't happen for a few years yet. But the final deadline for collecting the relevant data is fast approaching.*

*Maybe there's still time to take a field trip, to study the city of today in a more advanced incarnation.*

VOCE ESTÁ AQUÍ, the sign at the roadside rest stop declares, with unmistakable conviction. I don't know much of the language, but I've seen this declaration before—the same large, confident letters inked above a small red circle, perfectly concentric, on a subway map.

*YOU ARE HERE.*

It's comforting to find something of home in this place, this city even larger than the one I've come from several thousand miles away.

Maybe here they know where we're all heading.

I've come for the crowds, the congestion, but I rarely see hints of the whole of the city itself, the world's third largest, with eighteen million people. I had imagined something overwhelming, not the small bit of street and neighborhood through which I walk each day.

Where is everybody?

*VOCE E . . .*

The five letters have been traced in the film of dust that covers the back window of the car in front of me, driven by a middle-aged woman. She's zipping ahead, cutting in and out of traffic.

Does she know she's disappearing?

Too late.

She's gone before I can even hope to warn her.

I am told that it's almost impossible to conceive the city in its entirety. *You have to put the pieces together in your mind,* someone who has lived here for decades declares. He constructs his own city anew each day, one piece placed next to another, until he has what he needs at hand: sometimes just a street or two, sometimes a whole neighborhood.

*There's the place where I lived as a boy,* he says one afternoon, pointing to a house that's now hidden behind a high stone fence. We can't see anything at all as we drive by, but his eyes glow at the apparition.

*There's the square where my parents walked each evening before I was even born,* he reports a moment later, as he spies a few scraggly trees that seem to straighten ever so slightly as he passes.

And so it goes: not one but eighteen million cities, or more, constructed from scraps of memory and invention. Not so different, really, from what aficionados of the urban world have been doing for a long time.

*I have built this city for myself,* as a sixteenth century utopian once put it.

It's a skill you have to master if you really want to live here.

One day I am taken to view this vastness from the forty-first floor of a downtown office tower. It's a famously daunting vista, a kind of frisson for the traveler who may be sated on lesser forms of unfamiliarity.

Someone is already out on the walkway, trying to take pictures. *They say you can only see half of the city from here.* He's maneuvering his camera, twisting his head, attempting to cut absurdly truncated pieces out of the panorama.

He might as well have left his film at home.

I just look, lost in the landscape.

So this is the future: more than the human mind can hold, a fantastical contagion of concrete and brick. A hint of sky at the horizon, a few specks of green below, color dwarfed by an astonishing array of bony, bleached-out grays.

Each square foot is filled to overflowing. In the world to come, we won't need a word for *empty.*

✦     ✦     ✦

I am told that I shouldn't walk many places by myself. Everything is gated—all entrances at street level are barred, modest apartment buildings are barricaded, private homes hide themselves behind spindly iron fences, sentinels are posted on the street in better neighborhoods so that residents can walk from cars to doors under protective surveillance.

I'm not rich, but it's all relative. *You have more change in your pocket than most people here make in a month,* my host advises.

I take his admonitions seriously.

But it's easy to move out just a bit farther than one ought to, to slip past the perimeter and find oneself in a place where no one's watching, where anything can happen.

*Cuidado!* Be careful!

The phrase book I carry makes provision for all sorts of possibilities.

*Nao comprendo.* I do not understand.

*O que ha?* What is the matter?

*Fale mais devager, por favor.* Please speak more slowly.

*Perdi meus amigos.* I have lost my friends.

*Que devo fazor?* What am I to do?

On some level, all cities are much the same now.

*Nao comprendo. Que devo fazor?*

One week, I take a short trip from one city here to another.

I exchange smiles with my seatmate and glance at the pictures in the airline magazine. They're the only part of the publication that I can understand. Idly, I begin to study the safety card, something I recognize, and ponder whether the same busy person draws all those tilting planes and red arrows that always point straight at the ocean.

We've been aloft for almost twenty minutes before my seat-mate and I realize that we speak a common language.

He's an actor. He's here for a film, his first. He's excited about the trip, it's the most beautiful country he's ever seen, the farthest away he's ever been, but he's worried about the crime.

*Is it really as bad as they say?*

No, I assure him, it isn't that bad. At least nothing has happened to me.

*But just remember you've got more change in your pocket than most people here make in a month.*

He nods, as if that's bad enough.

Some time from now, when the film he hasn't yet begun to shoot is finally released, and judgments like *truly abhorrent* pepper at least one review, the young actor will discover a whole new dimension to worry. But for now he focuses, as most of us must, on the more imminent hazards of daily life.

Later, I learn that the murder rate here is actually on the rise, up to twenty-five killings a day. It's a new record, a kind of macabre milestone. Hundreds of violent robberies are also reported each day. And untold thousands of cars are stolen every week.

A highly placed religious figure has announced that it is morally acceptable, under certain conditions, to loot grocery stores if one is starving and in search of food. The president's wife concurs.

It's a delicate social calculus.

Another statistical watershed: over a thousand youths have recently escaped from two juvenile detention centers here.

It's news like this that really sets city people on edge.

It's one thing to consider the antisocial impulse abstractly, but altogether another to imagine legions of wayward avengers suddenly flooding the streets.

After all, these are children with nothing left to lose.

But some of the young people here are lucky, they're not lost, at least not yet. I think of the woman with the young boy who sits next to me on a park bench one afternoon. The heat is picking up. They've brought something to drink. I look off into the distance politely, but she turns and extends a plastic cup.

*Coca?*

And she encourages her son to pour a drink for the antisocial stranger.

Meanwhile, in a city not far from this one, the lovely resort to which the actor is en route, officials have adapted most adroitly to changing circumstances. Because carjackings are on the rise, with most occurring at stoplights after dark, a temporary edict has been issued: no driver need stop at a red light after ten P.M. Until further notice.

Or, as I might advise my anxious seatmate: *Just drive fast and don't slow down until the sun comes up.*

Who works in this city?

Not the one million applicants for the 10,000 positions that may open up at a bank. Or the 450,000 who hope to get 50,000 jobs sweeping the streets for a small but steady supply of money and food each month.

None of these wishful thinkers work in the city, at least not yet.

✦       ✦       ✦

But there are some who are always busy here:

The young girls who sell candies from car to car when traffic slows along the monstrous avenues that are threaded throughout the city.

Or the woman who simply walks with her newborn from driver to driver, the baby swathed in a piece of cloth that must have once been white.

Or the nimble boys who appear whenever a pileup occurs on the highway, bobbing and weaving through six lanes of traffic, hawking peanuts in little bags, the more serious the accident, the better the business.

Or the old man who can't move at all anymore, who stays put for hours and sells hot dogs (*Dogs do Tcham completo*) from the back of an ancient station wagon abandoned at the side of a street.

Or the three ladies who stroll the boulevard after midnight, waiting for cars to slow, hoping that some will stop. If the night isn't going well, the women will give up, hail a cab, and move on.

In a smaller coastal enclave, a villagelike settlement of only two million, one hears the high-pitched squeal of handicraft carts as they're trundled along the streets to market each day in midafternoon. The men who haul them are stone-faced and silent, but the carts complain, they don't want to work.

In that same little city I meet a young cabdriver.

He wants to learn English. He keeps an open dictionary beside him in the cab and speaks with exaggerated precision.

*Are you happy?*

I hardly know how to answer his question.

*My country is good only for rich,* he continues, practicing his pronunciation, slowly repeating the sentence.

It's one of the first he's learned in his new language, the language he hopes one day to speak in the glittering cities that beckon to him from afar.

Suddenly, I know all too well what ails him.

A sign I see here every so often: *RUA SEM SAIDA.* My dictionary translates it as *street without exit,* though I imagine we would call it *DEAD END.*

*Boa tarde,* I say one morning to a shopkeeper. She looks puzzled. I say it again—*B-o-a T-a-r-d-e*—pulling the phrase apart, like a piece of taffy, until it's nothing but vowels. It seems unnatural to me, a comical elongation, but she nods and smiles brightly: she understands.

I have a free afternoon, unexpectedly. *Use your time, go to the museum,* my anxious host suggests. But I simply want to walk around. He doesn't understand that the whole city is on display, though some sections show more of the curator's eye than others. But the most casual scene is compelling when seen for the first time.

The park: tall, slim trees with luxurious leaves, *fronds,* the word kept in reserve for just such occasions.

Five o'clock Mass: bells *pealing* (in other places, they would simply ring).

Squat buildings festooned with graffiti, impenetrable phrases suddenly become poetic in this lovely but indecipherable language.

Eventually I do visit the real museum, the one that charges admission.

I am especially taken with a piece of armor that once

belonged to a conquistador. How small a man he must have been, I think, it wouldn't fit anyone now.

I also study two pistols, Colt .45s, *Estados Unidos*: long dull silver barrels, worn wooden handles, heavy, old, the kind of gun no movie cowboy would ever use.

There's also a scale model of the museum itself on view, sitting in a small room of its own. The miniature version, the display placard informs us, took longer to construct than the monstrous full-sized building that surrounds us.

That makes sense, I think. It's natural to linger upon something one can see whole; it might almost be considered therapeutic.


Outside, on the streets, anomalous old houses from another century sit in forlorn splendor—delicate blocks of pinks, yellows, and greens that sparkle like stones placed in the wrong setting, threatened by the constant advance of urban construction.

The effort seems unending, seven days a week, from dawn to past dusk. Even on the most solemn day of the national calendar the city is busily replicating itself. Not everyone here can adjust to the new ways. *It's like your Thanksgiving,* someone from the old school says with indignation, as if the city can be shamed into slowing down.

Everywhere one hears the ringing of metal on metal, the screaming of electric saws, punctuated by occasional weak shouts of the workers. The rhythms of change are universal enough that a popular band has incorporated the effects into its show, tapping on hard hats with hammers and showering the darkened stage with sparks. Its audiences roar in recognition.

The new buildings seem to me like cigarette cartons placed on end, dozens of indistinguishable brands on display. But maybe I'm just searching for signs of the familiar in this other-worldly landscape.

Always, the construction is set in counterpoint to an ongoing process of decay, the city of the future decomposing before its very own eyes.

I'm waiting to meet someone for dinner at a club. It's fancier than anything I've experienced in my own circles; the red clay tennis surfaces are scrupulously brushed each evening, though the courts are usually empty, while people take cocktails on the terrace as the lesser royalty of England look on from their canvas perches. It's like something from *Life* magazine in the forties, I imagine, an oasis of privilege that seems utterly exotic to me.

I'm having my favorite drink, a national concoction made from something called *cachaca*. It's one word I'm likely to memorize.

The headwaiter has taken pains to make me comfortable while I wait. He gives me a fifteen-year-old *Reader's Digest* written in English, hesitantly, after I've been sitting for half an hour. I try to give it back, but he says *no, no, it's a gift.*

One more *caiperina* and I'm almost ready to read: "Five Myths That Can Wreck a Marriage"; "Walking—The Perfect Exercise."

The man and woman on the cover are frolicking (there's no other word for it in English) in the surf. They're dressed identically, white cotton pants, rolled up, with matching chartreuse sweaters. They wouldn't look out of place if they waded into this room.

After dinner, I try to give the *Digest* back again and get the same insistent *no, no, no.*

Later, someone will point the club out to me from the city's highest office tower. From up there it seems something of a supplicant, a tiny square of green muscled aside by grays.

A new trend: the well-to-do travel about the city in helicopters, far above the narrow, clotted corridors where ground traffic moves, if at all, in weak spurts.

There's no such sluggishness in the air.

Some liken the night sky here to strings of Christmas lights, moving at up to 130 miles per hour. It's a festive sight from afar, like the *favelas,* or slums, where the bare bulbs twinkle, after dark, as if bits of amber were scattered over the hillsides.

It's a kind of auroral extravaganza, one might say, at each economic extreme.

But not everyone approves of the affluent hovering above the rest of society.

*The desire for a helicopter,* one critic declares, *is a result of a complete lack of concern for other people.*

I want to visit a *favela,* but my host thinks the idea fantastically ill-considered. He can only shrug when he considers the subject.

*When the poor come down from the mountain* . . . It's a discreet observation, meant to leave something to the imagination, but it sounds to me like a song lyric that he's only half remembered.

Meanwhile, international financiers have issued a *wealth warning* to investors; there's a possibility that the economy here may falter even further, sending global stock markets into a spiral.

There are now about a billion truly poor people on the planet, mirrored by a billion others who resist the label "rich." Of course, they don't all live in the same city, not just yet.

If such a point comes to pass I expect we will see the earth and night sky both flare up, so that darkness becomes the scarcest of commodities in the city.

The most famous figure in this city is a totemic landmark known by sight around the world. Luminaries and ordinary folk alike make the pilgrimage to see it. My first night here I study the statue intently from the ground. It's easily visible from miles away, softly lit, glowing, majestic even in miniature.

When I see the landmark up close the next day I'm almost shocked. I hadn't expected to be spooked. The head seems huge, the eyes fierce and empty. There's nothing comforting about it; its hand alone would crush us if it fell.

When I gaze at it again from the ground, once more in miniature, it seems to me that the figure is trying to keep its balance, as if fighting off vertigo, or contemplating a suicidal dive off the cliff.

Maybe it can't handle its own immensity either.

A few months after my visit, in a story reported internationally, a young European will jump from the statue's outstretched arm in what the papers will describe as a *Bond-style stunt*.

His fall will take just two and a half seconds; he'll open his parachute at the last possible moment. But before he jumps an accomplice will take his picture, capturing for the world the image of a tiny figure perched, like a spindly insect, on the massive stone limb.

Back on the ground we pass a cemetery as we're driving

away. I can see a small copy of the statue, four feet high or so, reaching up to its hundred-foot likeness on the mountain above.

I think of an eighteenth century Asian city that once looked out upon a distant mountaintop its people considered sacred. They constructed a miniature scale model of the peak inside the city itself, enabling those who couldn't travel to make a pilgrimage of sorts, even so.

Someone in this cemetery, clearly, had a similar impulse.

But it wouldn't be the same, I suppose, for a modern-day pilgrim to jump from just four feet off the ground, to act in accord with what we call the *human scale*. No, it's much too late for that.

Who now would care to read about such a little leap?


I have been told that those who hold a college degree in this country, if imprisoned, are guaranteed by law a cell with a television set.

It sounds like an urban legend or, more precisely, a *factoid,* a provocative but inert bit of information that can't be linked, adroitly, to anything else.

It can only be passed on, in its solitary state, a story without much hope of a sequel.


I am also told that snakes captured anywhere in the country can be shipped from any train station, free of charge, to the world-renowned snake institute here. Experts in venomous snakes have developed several life-saving serums over the past hundred years. They're always on the watch for new species. They'll even provide the shipping crates.

Well, this cries out for connection.

A woman in the city I've come from found a long, thin paperlike strip of something in her apartment not long ago. She had the presence of mind to take it to someone for study. No doubt about it: it was the skin of a snake, probably a boa, at least ten feet in length.

Snakes, it seems, shed their skins in places where they feel comfortable.

She got what we call the *willies*. It was disturbing, the idea of something slithering around her, in the dark, while she was asleep. But people there don't move easily. She decided to conduct a thorough search for the thing and capture it.

But she couldn't find it, anywhere. No one could find it, not even the experts. Was it hiding in the walls? Under the floorboards? In the stove? No one could say.

At last report she was still looking.


I have ample opportunity in this exotic place to think about the purely accidental aspects of traveling, the random moments spent with people one will almost certainly never see again. Funny, it never strikes me as unusual when I experience it every day in the city.

Chance encounters:

• The Welsh couple who have been working for months in a dental clinic in the interior. They're lanky, relaxed, genial. The kind of people who seem always to have been together. They've raised two college-age sons and, along the way, devoted some years to volunteering in underdeveloped areas of the world.

She talks dreamily about floating under the jungle canopy, in a canoe, lying prone because the water level had risen so high. She wonders if beauty and indolence are fatefully intertwined.

He's perplexed. He sees only a grim future for this country, this continent, so much of the world he's tried, tooth by tooth, to redeem.

*Let's face it, the only colony that's ever been successful is America.*

Much later, I recount the conversation to people back home. The response is almost universal.

*What about Canada?*

• The Midwestern couple with two young children. His father was a missionary and he himself was born here, though he doesn't remember those exotic early years. He's a wiry man who wears a jaunty straw hat and a bright purple T-shirt on this hot, sun-drenched day.

He knows the language, talks to the people here with ease. There's something appealing about him. Maybe it's the easy smile, or the careless way he loops that hat around his neck.

We talk for a bit as our half-day tour travels from one little island to another.

Why has he come so far? He doesn't exactly know, his father isn't alive anymore, it has something to do with his own kids, the infant and giddy toddler who bounce around happily in the boat. He wants something more for them, he isn't sure quite what.

He makes an oblique reference to teenagers he never sees in the States. I'm surprised. He seems too young to have already shed an earlier life.

He wants to make his new wife happy. He had the kids for her, he says. He becomes quiet after making this admission.

She's changing a diaper. He goes off to help.

I watch him as he lurches to the back end of the boat, grabbing at ropes that sway in the wind, trying his best to keep his balance.

• The wary Canadian who's teaching a month-long seminar on agricultural law. She wants to change hotels, she isn't happy here, maybe it will be better on the beach. Maybe it won't. She's glad I've joined her for breakfast; she warns me to stay away from the eggs.

I wonder who I'm speaking to: the lonely traveler or the lawyer?

• The Western academic I meet at a dinner honoring his native-born wife. He's personable, the one who's been delegated to speak to me occasionally in English. Everyone at the party is cordial, but once we've exhausted our few common phrases we can only nod at one another. I've become childlike, smiling more broadly here than I ever do at home.

Conversations swirl about me, all elisions and guttural exhortations.

I make an observation to my conversational companion about cultural differences, the inevitability of isolation. It doesn't go over too well.

*You may be alone,* he declares, *but I'm not.*

I wonder for a moment if I've heard him right.

*Cuidado!* I can feel the smile fading.

*Sometimes traveling is like what used to be known as "tripping." The delirium, though willed, is strange, exhausting, stressful.*

*It's always wise to have a return ticket.*

✦    ✦    ✦

Once home, my own city seems more exotic than ever, almost clean, relatively uncrowded, even photogenic.

I see tourists with cameras, all taking the same shots, and I imagine the thousands of similar photographs that must exist at any given moment throughout the world. Some of them have been inserted carefully into albums, captioned in countless languages, others have probably been tossed, loosely, into musty boxes. In some cases, for sure, the film hasn't been developed yet.

It's an ancient impulse. We aren't satisfied simply with seeing, we want to hold on to what we have seen.

One day I see a young woman on the street flipping through small photographs, tiny rectangles of life telescoped together.

She's frozen in place, completely immersed in the pictures, as pedestrian traffic flows in eddies about her. Nobody seems the least curious about the cause of the obstruction.

Coincidentally, there's an exhibition at a city museum running at the same time: snapshots taken by city residents over the past fifty years, each meant to evoke associations of *home*.

In most of the pictures individuals pose for the camera, awkwardly, though a few display a saucy flamboyance. There aren't any candid shots that I can see. The photographer is usually a bit too far back, so that the figures are dwarfed by the domestic spaces enveloping them, or a bit too close, so that the small rooms seem cramped.

They're amateurish, which makes them appealing. No visual ingenuities here, just whatever the Brownie or Kodak or Polaroid can capture on its own.

The curators note that kitchen tables and TVs appear

throughout the thousand or so photographs that have been submitted to date, from which they've drawn some conclusions: *City people like to gather in kitchens, and everybody watches TV.*

I especially enjoy the shots taken in the forties and fifties. They're all in black and white, most just three-by-three, and they have a kind of modest containment that makes the bigger color shots of the sixties and later seem almost boastful.

But what's missing?

Always, the person taking the picture—at least one member of every family, tribe, or clan on view is lost to ritual sacrifice for the greater good.

Frowns: everyone smiles in these pictures, even the kids.

Streets: only interiors are featured, as if the city is hiding from itself.

Those who live alone: the ones who can't take pictures of themselves represent the invisible demographic in this display.

There is, as it happens, one picture in the exhibit without a trace of a person in it, excluding the few that feature cats; it was taken by a fellow who suffers a professed fetish for old objects. Here he shows off wooden ironing boards, toys, and metal tins.

Wait—there's something human here after all in the idiosyncrasy on view.

But most people in the city don't send their pictures to museums, much less have them matted and mounted on a wall for all to see.

Most are like the old woman on the subway who sorts through several shots until she fixes on just one. I can hardly make it out: two, no, three women, their hair whitened, posing on a patio with extravagant plants and vines curling around them on a trellis.

There's greenery everywhere—isn't that a bit of grassy backyard in the far corner?

She looks at this image for a very long time; she's put the others aside.

She isn't really on the subway, she isn't even in the city, as long as she's lost herself in the picture.


How could one hold on to the city before the advent of the photograph?

I've read of a popular Japanese printmaker in the nineteenth century who lived in what was then the world's largest city, with a million or so residents. He was a fireman—when the wooden city wasn't burning, as it often was, he worked at his art while waiting for the next tiny spark to catch and spread.

He virtually invented the idea of the urban perspective. You might say he was one of the first to look at the city. Or one of the first who couldn't look away.

His masterwork, completed late in his life, consists of one hundred views of the city, each exquisitely composed.

Each color of the finished print was applied in separate sweeps over a hand-carved wooden surface, a technique acquired after a painstaking apprenticeship. It wasn't like taking one hundred photographs, changing, say, four rolls of film. It took a lifetime to capture these fleeting shots.

I saw the luminous images almost accidentally. when I happened to read that a museum only half a mile away was exhibiting a rare first edition for the second time in seventy years. I had just six days left to see it.

The colors are bright and pure, even in the dim light of the exhibition hall.

The famous images are here—the farmers, boatmen, courtesans, revelers flying delicate, colorful kites.

But the most startling element of the exhibition is the perspective on display—the views are oblique, off center, provisional, and some images are unmistakably incomplete by conventional pictorial standards.

In one print, a geisha is seen only in shadow; in another, three figures look out at something that we cannot see, our view blocked by a tree; in another, a famous shrine that should be the focal point of the print is obscured by a plume of gray smoke that rises in its center; in street scenes, the figures walk away from us, so that we see only the backs of their heads; and in scenes sketched through windows, the latticework of the wooden frame cuts the cityscape up into pieces.

The most famous image of the group depicts six figures dispersing in a sudden storm: parasols and papers serve as umbrellas, thin black slashes of rain slice the picture into diagonal strips.

How can one put it? He possessed a gift for showing us not so much what we see, but how those of us who live in the city see it. He was a master of *ukiyo-e*, the art of the floating world.

The city floating into awareness, then floating away: that seems a fitting way to conceive it.

In some translations, the phrase is rendered *sad world*. That seems fitting as well.

Some of his countryman today, during a yearly festival in the far north, carve life-sized buildings out of towering blocks of ice and snow. The structures stand for only a week. In years past, they've recreated the Taj Mahal and a number of European palaces. Scale and detail are to be rendered exactly; if something isn't quite right, they start over again, working against the weather. They know their time is limited.

*Ukiyo-e:* wooden cities burn, snow cities melt, as they have, and will, forever.

One summer night the usually sober city throws itself a party, promising to deploy one hundred fifty tons of fireworks. I'm awaiting the display in a penthouse apartment overlooking the harbor, along with a small group of revelers who usually live, as I do, at a lower elevation.

The city seems almost carelessly striking at this altitude. The explosives, when they finally ignite, will have to compete with the thousands of tiny lights firing up, as they do every evening, in suddenly flamboyant buildings, each one a diva expecting its due.

A woman at the party, tipsy, knocks an empty tumbler off the terrace. We can hardly see it as it falls the twelve or so stories. Experts have proven that a penny thrown from the tallest building in the city will never hit the ground. But no one's done the work on clear plastic cups; for all we know it could land, like a missile, half a block from here. Or maybe it will sway, lightly, taking its time as it floats downward in a more or less harmless descent.

We do know that many valuable discoveries have been made quite accidentally, as when someone leaves a dirty petri dish in the lab at the end of a day and finds an entirely new compound under the microscope the next morning. This might be no different. We simply have to study the city, *in vitro,* whenever the opportunity arises.

The festive strangers on the street below never break their stride. They seem unaware of the menace above them. Several seconds pass, enough time for some response to register, but we see nothing unusual at all. Their zigzagging doesn't seem to be defensive.

Barring further evidence, we have no choice but to term our impromptu experiment *inconclusive.*

One day, our newspaper prints a picture of old mail-order houses that still stand in a small town in the Midwest. They were packaged and shipped for assembly in the early 1900s by a well-known national department store.

*They're good starter homes,* a current occupant observes, though you may have to stay put in your little house years after your family has outgrown it, as hers has, because you can't afford to move out.

And so city mice and country mice learn they have something in common.

I've got that store's catalog in front of me now; it's only twelve years old, but already extinct, the last of its kind. Nothing here can be ordered anymore; it's a tantalizing display of the unattainable.

A kind of *ur–wish list,* if you will.

In page after page one finds washers, dryers, hot water heaters, all the serious appliances that even a farceur could never squeeze into a city apartment.

✦      ✦      ✦

Want a ping-pong table? It's here. Beekeeping equipment? Best to put that on the porch. Twelve years ago, you could buy a queen bee for $8.99. For another $20, you could get six thousand worker bees as well.

And there are over a hundred pages of items that are meant to go into a *garage*. Some of us here have seen these large, cluttered appendages to living spaces, if only on television.

It seems I'm not the only one who's been reading a catalog.

A family in a brownstone across the way has begun to barbecue every weekend, sometimes in the rain, on a little deck that floats, like a rickety wooden raft, two stories off the ground.

Someone else has placed lawn chairs and a hibachi on the roof of a nearby building.

Two old men at street level sit in vinyl chairs outside for hours on a few square feet of cement.

On a weekend evening in summer, the smell of roasted meat wafts over the entire neighborhood, as if a mysterious suburban metamorphosis has occurred.

And it's not just here: I've seen people in third world cities crouched over open fires, beneath highways, cooking while shivering in an autumn chill. They could have used a grill, page 236. Or a tent, page 280, *endorsed by the man who climbed Mt. Everest.*

As for me, I'm keeping the catalog handy.

It's a sultry day, the kind of day where we're warned to stay indoors and most everyone goes outside anyway. People move slowly in the thick air; even the babies are too sluggish to squirm. An ambulance pulls away as I pass the local hospital, while another one, lights flashing, drives up. There's refuge from heatstroke inside.

I get a postcard. It's from someone very far away.

*I think you would enjoy it here. You should come.*

There isn't much of a clue on the card itself as to where "here" is. I can't place the name of the writer either, and the lapse is beginning to bother me. Surely I know him. He certainly knows me.

For a moment, I flounder, and then from the fringes of memory I retrieve a face and name to match. Of course. He promised to write. Most people don't follow through in that way; no wonder I was thrown.

If he had indicated a return address, I'd send him a response.

*Still here. Bring ice if you ever come back.*


What else has been lost?

Experts tell us that half of the world's six thousand languages will disappear in years to come, once the last few speakers of the endangered dialects have passed away.

We won't have twenty-five synonyms for snow anymore. Who knows, in time we may lose the word for *winter.*

Already, it seems, there is less to say. *I cannot tell my dreams to anyone,* one old woman remarks, haltingly, in the new language she has just begun to learn, the language without nuance, the city language that drifts in over the radio, and television, and into every corner of the countryside, so that she resists its advances only when she sleeps.

In her dreams she speaks freely, if only to herself.

✦     ✦     ✦

Here's something else to worry about: what if 911 were to fail?

It's already happened, actually, several times this year. Agitated callers have experienced excruciating delays—fifteen, twenty, thirty seconds—before reaching someone on the other end, time enough for even the most tenuous sort of trouble to take root.

One day, the system simply shut down for an hour. The sirens were silent, the fire trucks and ambulances almost aimless.

Who knows how many shots were fired, hearts seized up, mattresses set to smolder in those sixty minutes?

And all that while the rest of us weren't even aware that anything was wrong.

It's as if all the languages of the world had been reduced to one word, *help,* and there was nobody left to hear it.

Current thinking on mischance and cataclysm:

Research reveals that in the first phase of disaster, that misleading lull known in the literature as the warning period, most people experience *the inhibition of tendencies toward flight.*

They simply don't believe that anything is going to happen.

But that's the most dangerous moment, when the O-rings begin to erode, or the brake locks as you near the icy intersection, or the wind that swirls in the distance settles into the form of a funnel.

Maybe it's an April night in the North Atlantic, or maybe you're eleven miles from safety at the South Pole.

Suddenly you're shivering from the chill in the air. And it will only get colder, because nothing can save you now.

Even if you should, by chance, survive.

✦     ✦     ✦

*If I had been at Pompeii . . .*

Would I have taken advantage of the moment and studied the crisis as it was unfolding? Or would I have panicked and run as the waves of volcanic ash began to engulf the city?

It would have been impossible to see anything in the sudden darkness. But who would have wanted to watch?

It was all over in a matter of minutes.

Some of the fossilized figures are caught in midstride, their mouths open; others are curled up as if hoping somehow to hide.

The city is suspended in time too, the skeletal remains of stone walls and houses still crowding the empty streets. Hard to believe it was buried for eighteen hundred years. The ruins, uncovered quite inadvertently, now draw new crowds: visitors drawn to the moment of catastrophe itself, captured almost cleanly, like an ancient insect in amber.

It's the embodiment of what worries us most—*THE END*—arriving without any possibility of preparation or appeal.

*If I had been on the* Hindenburg . . .

It is the largest airship of its era, 804 feet long, hovering only a few hundred feet above the earth.

When it floats across the countryside, or the sea, it draws its own languorous shadow in its wake.

The sight causes spectators on the ground to smile; when the ship glides over cities, people run to the roofs of tall buildings and wave.

I probably would have been waving too, wishing I could take the marvelous ride myself. After all, what could possibly go wrong?

✦     ✦     ✦

Fact: the fireball begins to flame in the rear and moves with horrific rapidity, so that the silvery skin of the dirigible, thin as paper, is consumed in a few minutes, while the aluminum bracing underneath melts into a twisted mass. Hundreds have come simply to watch the ship land, but suddenly they're on the run, scattering like errant sparks thrown off from the molten remains.

Many will escape. But for the rest of their lives they will reprise this one moment.

They will be engulfed, finally, by the force of the story itself.

*If I had been in Johnstown . . .*

It's one thing to worry about fire, but who has reason to be wary of water?

Only, perhaps, those who have made their home in a nineteenth century city that lies in a valley with a dam some miles upstream. If it should rain one May week, and keep on raining, it might rain so much that lifelong residents will swear they've never seen the likes of it: *I never knew of so much rain to fall in such a short time.*

If it rains that much, the ground will soften up until it's swollen.

Some will hardly sleep, unusually restless, though they do not yet know why. *I was wakened up during the night by the noise of the rain.*

But by four P.M. the next day the whole town will be uneasy, dimly sensing the residual effect of all that rain, the twenty million tons of water that will course through the crack in the dam, causing its weakened walls to crumble, flooding the valley below.

The wave that does most of the damage will be fifty or so feet high, and hundreds of feet wide.

It will only take ten minutes. Wooden structures will splinter into toothpicks; trees that have stood for years will be torn up by the roots and tossed aside. A train will hang tenuously on its trestle, *swinging around like a string of beads,* until it breaks apart.

It will seem as if some sullen giant, tired of play, has morosely smashed his toys.

*They had to make good speed to get out, and if they couldn't make it, they were lost.*

Hundreds will forever be listed as missing, among them four sisters—Viola, Sarah, Ida, and Ella—and an infant sibling six weeks old who never received a name, along with seven members of another family—Charles, Adolph, Maggie, Rose, and Mary, and their parents Constantine and Frances.

Word of the disaster will spread throughout the nation in newspapers, avidly snapped up, the event prompting the largest circulation boost since the assassination of the president some twenty-five years earlier.

Within five years the city will be rebuilt by the survivors. But no one who lived through that moment will ever forget it. *I never saw anything like that in all my life before anywhere, and I was raised along the water.*

Could it be that nature itself bears an animus against the city?

In some, urban aversion emerges almost at birth.

A painter renowned for his pristine images of country life was born in the city, living here only a few years, but long

enough to collect the impressions that would color his recol-
lections for the rest of his life.

*It all depends on how you see it,* he once remarked.

He remembered as a little boy looking out from rooftops
upon the dirty clutter of city life, open lots and alleys littered
with cans, bottles, stray tufts of grass scattered in ragtag
clumps. Sometimes he saw drunken couples clawing at each
other on the street. Once, a corpse on the sidewalk. Even the
snow, as it fell, blackened with soot.

There must have been prettier pictures, but he simply didn't
see them.

The country, in his recollection, was sunny; the city, even
fifty years later, *sordid, filthy, gloomy, smutty.*

Worse yet, it was *complicated.*


But for a brief period in his life he had imagined painting a
radiant city.

As a young artist he mounted a map of Paris on his studio
wall and studied it for a whole summer, committing its intrica-
cies to memory, walking its imagined boulevards and precincts
many times over in his mind. *Rue Bonaparte, Jardin du
Luxembourg, Pont de la Concorde,* lustrous names worn down
to the nub by the press of his imagination.

But he never made that trip.

We remember him now for the hundreds of covers he
painted for the most widely read magazine of his day. It is a
world of swimming holes and wood-paneled station wagons,
where colors and shapes work in concert, a whole story conveyed in an irrepressibly neat package.

He was always aware of his limits.

He knew that he could never smooth out the ragged edges of a city picture, that there is no such thing as a simple city story.

Someone else who bore ill will toward the city: a nineteenth century philosopher-naturalist who fled the settled world to live by a pond. His handcrafted cabin was tiny, not much bigger than a roomy birdhouse.

He renounced the technologies of the day, finding no use for speed, convenience, or distraction. The new railroad, in particular, irked him.

He didn't think much of the newspaper either.

Most of his contemporaries found his strange ways inexplicable. It was a case of mutual wonderment. *I have never met a man who was quite awake,* he avowed. But he had aroused the curiosity of the townspeople around him. They had questions.

How could he live in the middle of nowhere?

Wasn't he ever at loose ends? Wasn't he ever lonesome?

Yes, once, for a moment, on a rainy evening, when the surrounding woods seemed altogether too dark and empty. It was an unfamiliar feeling, something to be studied rather than resisted. *I was conscious of a slight insanity in my mood, and seemed to foresee my recovery.* In time, as he had hoped, the moment passed and he was himself once again.

But his listeners weren't satisfied with just a few stories. They wanted to know more. He wrote a book.

He had read the *Vishnu Purana* and sometimes, he told his readers, he prepared for the Visitor Who Never Comes, the guest whose arrival is said to be imminent. The ancient ritual of hospitality had been passed down over millennia of communal life. One was to wait in patient readiness for one's guest. On many occasions, on those evenings when the woods seemed especially close, he sat expectantly at his door.

He notes that no such visitor ever approached. He doesn't tell us whether he was truly disappointed.

Eventually he left the wilderness. His primer still sells handily today, especially in the city.

Sometimes discontented individuals actively resist the urban environment, so much that they try to blow it up, bit by bit, as in the case of the bomber who strikes sixteen times over the course of seventeen years, evading detection with ease.

He sends some of his bombs through the mail.

But others are hand-placed in hallways, on tables, in parking lots, just sitting, unobtrusively, waiting patiently for some curious person to pick them up.

The city, he knows, is full of curious people.

Sometimes the lifting action alone triggers the detonation. Sometimes, one has to untie the parcel, take out the seemingly harmless book or three-ring binder or cigar box inside, and open that up.

Then a roar, a flash, a whiff of smoke, homemade shrapnel spiraling through the air.

No one ever sees the agent, just the residue, meticulously cataloged by the experts who slowly sift through it: *nails, screws, remnants of redwood, two types of powders, five types of tape* . . .

There are no prints to be found.

It seems that the bogeyman himself is making the lethal deliveries.

✦     ✦     ✦

The FBI develops a profile of the bomber. They're looking for a recluse, a highly organized hermit who dresses neatly. He may have trouble with women. He likes to make lists. He's probably a quiet fellow who would make an ideal neighbor.

Unless he's not acting alone. In which case he might be one of several neighbors, a coterie of antisocial individuals who have banded together in spite of themselves.

People throughout the country subsequently read the profile and take a new look at friends and acquaintances. Suspicions begin to arise. Some openly wonder about family members.

The prime suspect's mother will later admit that she recognized someone much like her own boy in the hypothetical depiction. But she knew in her heart that her child could never do such a thing.

It must be someone else's son.

Universities, prime targets of the bombings, distribute cautionary fliers to campus personnel. They're adorned with crude drawings of suspicious packages and envelopes. Professors and staff are instructed to watch out for items wrapped with too much string, or stray wires sticking out, or odd discolorations, or bits of tinfoil protruding from the paper. Maybe the address is old, or the package is marked *Personal*. Recipients are urged to refuse unexpected mail.

*Remember—It May Be a Bomb*.

But none of the elaborate precautions seem to slow the pace of the incidents or flush the fellow out.

✦     ✦     ✦

One day, in a small western city, someone is seen placing a device on the ground near a woman who happens to be looking out a window. She calls to a coworker, loudly enough so that the man turns and looks straight at her. He remains still for a moment, then hurries away. He leaves his package behind.

An hour later someone else, unsuspecting, picks it up.

The man's face, the eyewitness will later recall, seemed expressionless. But the resulting sketch of the suspect based on the single glimpse she got becomes infamous. Everyone keeps an eye out for the figure in the drawing, the face half hidden beneath a hooded sweatshirt.

The scare is enough to keep even the bomber from spooking the city for almost six years.

But eventually the recluse reemerges. He compels a national newspaper to publish a thirty-six-thousand-word manifesto, 252 precisely numbered paragraphs of cultural critique. He's aggrieved; he thinks the industrial world order cripples the spirit. He extols the healing nature of rural life. He wonders about the wisdom of an unexamined march toward modernization.

So far, he might almost be said to be making some sense.

But one sentence, deep within the manuscript, just sits there, ticking away.

*In order to get our message before the public with some chance of making a lasting impression, we've had to kill people.*

BOOM!

In a single moment the message, whatever its merits, shatters into thousands of twisted sentences, phrases, and syllables, beyond any hope of reconstruction.

Like many a city story, as it happens.

✦　　✦　　✦

Ultimately, the bomber is incriminated through stylistic tics in his own writings, the odd wordings and obsessions that echo through decades' worth of documents. His personal papers will be archived in a collection of anarchist materials housed in a major university library.

The city isn't about to be caught unawares again.

In the course of an investigative postmortem the authorities compile a dossier of every known document relating to the suspect. His life, it seems, is a puzzle, a mystery awaiting resolution by those willing to immerse themselves in the painstaking work of divination. They labor through thousands of receipts and records until a portrait materializes before them.

It turns out he's brilliant, a self-starter who fled the city for the woods. He lived in a cabin he built by himself, plank by plank, with no running water or electricity. The cabin will eventually be trucked, whole, to an FBI warehouse in another state.

It's about the size of his prison cell, or a small studio apartment.

Research also reveals that he couldn't read the newspaper regularly, he found that the stories upset him, aroused anxieties that even his soothing self-imposed isolation could not entirely dispel.

Maybe he had more in common with city folk than he could ever imagine.

Maybe he, too, is a quintessential city person.

After his capture, a rural librarian will speak almost warmly of the familiar figure now outfitted in a bright orange jail jumpsuit. She likes him. He used to talk to her, hesitantly, as he worked at his research. Once, he helped out at a library open house.

He was the only person who ever requested back issues of *Scientific American*.

Anyone could see he had some ambition.

One last bomb is found in the cabin, fully assembled, ready for delivery. It lacks only an address. But the bogeyman won't be making any more mail runs.

And some lucky city fellow will never receive the inviting package marked *Personal*.


Not everyone who wants to get away from it all is a malevolent loner.

But what can one do in the modern, impossibly over-crowded world? How does the city dweller today find space, solace, peace?

One young man has devised his own way to achieve something resembling serenity. He lives in a single room in the city, not much bigger than a cell or a cabin in the wilderness would be. The rest of his immigrant family shares the cramped space with him. But the boy escapes when he needs to.

*When I want to be alone,* he says, *I just close my eyes.*

It's better than building a bomb, and something like writing a book.


There are others, mutants of a sort, who are temperamentally suited to the city. Indeed, one can hardly imagine them living anywhere else.

One day a twenty-something girl sits next to me on the sub-way, swathed in black, with a wedge of cropped blond hair that accentuates the monochromatic look. She takes out a lined tablet and begins to scribble at a furious pace, filling six pages as I watch. Surreptitiously, I glance at what she's writing, but the text is unintelligible. For all I can tell, she might be working in another medium altogether—it could be a drawing, a sketch, a miniature mockup of a larger mural that she's working on in a small cramped studio downtown.

Meanwhile, the inky black lines continue to spill out onto the pages with a kind of crazed fluidity.

Eventually I make out one shaky mark, little more than a slash, that seems to be repeated at regular intervals. Suddenly it makes sense: it's the first-person pronoun, *I*, thrown out like an anchor into the torrent of thought.

So it's a text after all, but only its author can read it.

A day later I happen to sit next to a young woman who's studying a book in what seems to be a hieroglyphiclike language.

What kind of story is she reading? It's impossible to tell. All I can identify are the numbers in the margins.

She's on page 323.

*You like lists,* someone tells me.

*Guilty as charged,* I confess.

I hadn't really thought about it, one slips into one's obsessions. But it isn't the prospect of order that I find appealing, my lists are far more likely to be assembled with haphazard élan, more or less at random.

No, it's the power of distillation, the modest pleasure of whittling the known world down until only the smallest of slivers remain, arranged in crisp rows or columns. But I can't claim to have started a trend—no one wants to read thick, heavy books anymore, the tomes that once were labored over for a lifetime.

We'd rather skim headlines now.

It may be an evolutionary adjustment; as all those open fields and lots fill up, across the planet, there just isn't room left to stack cumbersome volumes.

The changeover will take some time. In the transitional phase, books will be digitized, then carried around on disks in backpacks and pockets. But even radical shrinkage is simply a stopgap measure.

Soon enough, we'll need to adjust to widespread scarcity—space, time, expressive capacities themselves will all be in very short supply. The practice of writing will dwindle; reading itself may be rationed.

At that point we'll need to reorient ourselves more radically if we hope to resist the extinction of the text.

We'll need a new technique.

Something lean and pithy.

Something like a list.

You might say that the list is the *art form of the future*. And that some prescient person in the city, ignored by his neighbors, pitied by his friends, driven only by dim intuition, is almost certainly whittling away at a short masterwork even now.

Fact: after months of investigative dead ends, a long-sought arsonist is finally arrested here to widespread relief. He was seen hovering on the fringes of three fires that broke out in a matter of hours—like someone in a theme park who's purchased a one-day pass to all the attractions. Someone became suspicious; once the fellow was confronted, he owned up to the deeds easily.

They think he started eighteen fires throughout the city. These last three were set in his own neighborhood. Maybe he was tiring of all the travel.

But not all firebugs are eager for recognition.

Take the woman who owned the cow that kicked over the lantern that started the fire that leveled much of a great nineteenth century city.

That conflagration consumed eighteen thousand buildings. The barn was the first to go; legend has it that the cow's mistress was doing her milking at the time, but she swore she was fast asleep when the fire first broke out. At the formal hearing that ensued, she claimed to have been as surprised as anyone, maybe more flustered than most.

*I got the way I did not know when I saw everything burn up in the barn. I got so excited that I could not tell anything about the fire from that time.*

Indeed, her neighbors were possibly less vigilant than she, dancing and fiddling into the night. *I could hear them from my bedroom. Could hear them going on. There was a little music there.*

Who, she might almost have suggested, was the likelier villain: a dour, hardworking, simple woman, or a giddy young boarder who dances?

Smart move, but too little, too late: the story had already chosen its main character.

A hundred years later, the cow and its owner will be exonerated, more or less, but the myth of their misdeeds will live on in urban lore. Most people, if queried, will blame them both, as if to acknowledge that a good story isn't always fueled by the facts.

Fact: selected images from commercial spy satellites have recently been targeted at urban planners. There's a market, it's thought, for information about cities that can be gathered through aerial surveillance.

One test image was shot from four hundred miles in space and shows an intersection in a major urban area, with unsuspecting city folk caught on camera as they drive just a bit too fast, hoping to beat the light.

The astoundingly precise instrument is able to reveal small objects from its vantage point in space—buildings, cars, clumps of vegetation.

But not, for some reason, people. They're harder to render. So the image will show the dangling seat belt, but not the lazy driver who's disdained it.

Private industry plans to sell these images for as little as $30 per square mile.

While thinking about the ambitious enterprise I recall a question someone once asked that I couldn't, at the time, answer: *why is everyone who's ever seen a UFO always a lousy photographer?* The evidence seemed irrefutable, once I thought about it: all those blurry, light-tinged blob shapes hovering in the sky, shrouded in darkness, over the desert. No one who knew anything about f-stops or adequate exposures would compose pictures under such conditions.

But now I wonder: what if the premise of the question itself is faulty? Maybe it's in the nature of alien objects to be indistinct, perhaps it's only the inhabitants of earth who strive for higher resolution, sharper edges, ever greater clarity.

*A modern city lives by the straight line,* an influential architect once told us.

His ideas, dominant for years, were in time abandoned for the chaotic urban accretion that he abhorred. But the residual traces of such rectilinear thinking can be seen today in the designs of cities all over the world.

He would never have welcomed fuzzy extraterrestrials into his ideal city. Such creatures, intelligent enough to monitor earthly communications, aware of the latest idée fixe, would naturally assume that they ought to arrive by stealth, in the dead of night, in the least populated areas of the planet, while no one was watching.

No wonder they went to the desert. They didn't know the truth, that one could land at high noon in the center of the city, sparks flying, and still have to vie for attention.

A space phenomenon of perhaps greater interest to urban planners: the newspaper has recently announced the successful testing of a lifeboat for an international space station that is currently under construction.

The rescue craft was jettisoned at thirty-nine thousand feet and left to tumble toward the earth; its parachutes opened as hoped and it landed without incident.

*We purposely put in some pitches and rolls,* a proud engineer remarked.

But isn't there an even more urgent use for such a lifesaving device?

One could conceive of a rescue craft that isn't meant to land but remains in orbit, suspended, a sanctuary for refugees from the ailing earth cities so infinitely far below it.

We might need such an outpost, eventually.

The present design, however, will only accommodate seven people at a time. At that rate, we would require over a million pods for our current population, and millions more for other urban areas as they develop.

It's a challenge, for sure.

But someone has to build the floating cities of the future.

✦     ✦     ✦

Who else is lost?

Perhaps the old man in the old story who went hunting one day in the woods, met a stranger, had a drink, and fell into a fateful sleep. When he awakens his rifle is rusted, his dog (though he doesn't know it) long since dead, the village he returns to altered in every aspect, people far less friendly than before, his own house gone to ruin.

Twenty years had passed in that one night.

It seems a diabolical compression of experience, a cruel thing for a writer to do to his own character, throwing him into a foreign setting, turning him into a stranger, shaken by change, oppressed by surprise.

No wonder he felt bewitched. And possibly just a bit excited.

What had happened? It's not so inexplicable, actually, from a contemporary perspective. We have the concepts now to explain such a metamorphosis.

It's simple: he fell asleep in a town and awoke to find himself in a city.

Who might be most lost of all?

Maybe the one who keeps searching for something, long past the point where others would have given up looking. Someone who can't *get out while the going is good,* who wouldn't know how to turn back if he had to.

Someone, that is, like the seventeenth century explorer who was the first to sail up the city river that now grandly bears his name. He remapped much of the known world in his time, but that accomplishment counted, in his eyes, for almost nothing. He made four fruitless voyages from the old to the new world in search of a shortcut, a sea passage that would open to Europe the riches of the East.

At least that was the nominal cause of his curiosity. But it isn't much of a motive, not one that accounts for the third attempt, or the fourth. He was said to have been obsessed, even dangerously unmindful of his own well-being, not the kind of person who's simply in it for the money.

His arduous voyages are now rendered, four hundred years on, as simple childish lines—red, green, purple, pink—that someone has drawn in an atlas.

It's easy to be matter-of-fact about what went awry. One can see the missteps on the map. Here he's taken a wrong turn; there he's heading straight into an Arctic ice pack. He caroms from one landmass to another, touches coastlines as if he were playing tag.

He isn't even close to the open sea he seeks, though he doesn't know that as he sails into his watery cul-de-sac.

It seems he's playing blind man's bluff as well.

On the last voyage, they think he lost his nerve and chose to hug the coast as a cold winter closed in.

He was finally overpowered by a mutinous crew that was tired and weak and wanted to go home. He didn't want to go with them. They marooned him in a small open boat, along with his son and a few others, and left him on his own as the mother ship sailed off.

That was the last anyone ever saw of him. An X marks the spot on the map where the trail stops.

We don't even know what he looked like; he left no portrait behind.

But it seems to me he was a born city boy—quixotic, edgy, always on the verge of losing his way in something much larger. Maybe he would have found his bearings if the city had only been here when he first entered the harbor.

At the very least, he would have found his wondering gaze reflected in thousands of city faces.

My high school history teacher once made a notation, in red, under an epigraph that I had chosen for a paper: *Source is obviously the Constitution; why not say so?* Curiously, it wasn't a command, or a simple instruction. He was asking the question as if there might be more than one answer, and so you could say that he taught me something he probably hadn't intended to.

It's a lesson I've always remembered. It might be put this way: *nothing can ever be nailed down.* What's obvious to one person is unclear to another, what we think we know is subject always to amendment, we'll use words like *probably* and *maybe* more often, if we're truthful, than we can ever imagine when we're just starting out.

But it may be that I have fashioned this rationale entirely after the fact. I've got a theory, that's all, to explain an impulse that will always remain something of a mystery to me.

Why not just say so?

One evening, decades on, I find myself standing beside someone on the subway who seems to be a teacher. He appears to be correcting a student essay on *Oedipus Rex*. It's a classic, of course, though I'm surprised that high school students still read it. But what better introduction to being blindsided, to learning of all that can happen to a life when you aren't looking?

The Greeks, after all, knew something about wreckage.

The writer begins boldly, making a reference to *Fate's master plan for Oedipus*. Her handwriting is neat, careful, the blue words marching obediently from one margin to the other. Every so often, a tentative parenthesis or hyphen appears, as if she feels the need to explain herself as clearly as she can.

He's reading quickly, his red pen poised lightly above each line. Every so often a mild reproof is jotted beside a suspect phrase. He's asking questions—*Relevance? Thesis?*—that seem unpromising to me.

I only catch fragments of her analysis on the last page, but I can see that she's got a strong windup.

*Overall, I don't believe in going to an Oracle—live normally without knowing what will come is easier.*

He finishes correcting the grammar and gives her a D-minus on the draft.

I'm taken aback. I imagine a girl who's sitting in an apartment somewhere in this vast, uncertain city, struggling to sustain a capacity for surprise, wondering if it makes any sense at all to ask *why?* Good for you, I think—give up the need for omniscience now and just plunge right into your story.

From what I saw of her work, I would have given her a higher grade.


A question I ought to have asked much earlier: just what is a fact? Is it something cold, hard, unforgiving, the kind of thing that tight-lipped men and women mete out in careful measure? Or is it something more malleable, even amenable, almost cheerfully changing its nature according to how we choose to see it?

Experts, of course, can argue either way.

Legal minds routinely refer to the idea of a *fact pattern,* as if to say that bits of experience ought to be woven together. Laymen too like to speak of facts in the plural, knowing there's safety in numbers.

Maybe we sense that a fact, left on its own, is unsettled, at loose ends, even lonely. But who would want to own up to such an admission?

It would threaten the distinction we've so adamantly drawn between matters of fact and feeling.


So how many facts have I gathered so far? How many more would it take to tell the whole tale?

I suspect that I could collect these strands forever, link one discrete element to another, extend the narrative indefinitely, and still it would seem incomplete. There would always be something else to remark upon, something else to say.

Maybe that's why the idea of sending a telegram was once so appealing: *a few words, STOP, a few more, STOP,* it's finished, send it off.

But that doesn't allow for the happy accident, the pursuit of one idea, the abrupt discovery of something else. One ought to get lost in thought, at least occasionally, it keeps the story supple.

So when will the story be finished? Perhaps when I simply write STOP.


Who still reads a newspaper?

Self-confessed cultists, devotees of antique technologies? The hopelessly out of date?

As it happens, I'm still studying a headline from a hundred-some years ago: *Edison's Electric Light: Conflicting Statements as to Its Utility.*

The inventor himself, it seems, insisted on demonstrating his device only to practical men who possessed *horse sense;* he would have nothing to do with dreamers.

This from the man who experimented with hundreds of prototypes before he found a filament that wouldn't burn up in a matter of seconds.

There he was, trying to persuade hard-boiled nonbelievers to see the future as he saw it.

Of course, they couldn't see the earth from space, as we can, its cities lit up at night, its rural areas invisible from that distance in the dark. A practical man might be frightened at the sight, the world on fire and no easy way to extinguish it.

Just this month, a new headline, heralding *A New Era:* scientists have mapped the human genetic code. Useful metaphors abound in the accounts: it's *an instruction book, a blueprint, a manual of life itself.* Several full pages of the paper are devoted to the discovery; it seems that mankind has achieved *a pinnacle of human self-knowledge.*

Anyone with horse sense can see it.

Meanwhile, some wish to reinvent the newspaper so that it might survive the technological tsunami that's fast approaching. They've convened a conference. I say they ought to invite the dreamers, the ones still drawn to the disjunct stories and casual epiphanies that more practical folks toss out at the end of every day.

The ones who could tell them that it's not the technology but the state of mind that matters.

A conference of thoroughly impractical people who might look into the future, blindly, without flinching.

✦     ✦     ✦

Science conjectures that only the fittest survive, that *inferior individuals* fall by the wayside as the species marches on.

A harsh judgment, no doubt. But it might be useful to close our study with a look at those we call, if unkindly, *the unlucky,* a subset of the maladapted. They're the ones who almost made it, who came agonizingly close to what one would consider a happy ending.

*Things have come out against us,* a British explorer of the last century reported when he found himself, against expectation, facing sure extinction. He wasn't supposed to freeze to death, he must have thought, as he wrote a few last lines to the world with a stub of a pencil, waiting alongside his icy companions for the onset of unconsciousness.

In the end, he declared, they had come *very near to great success.*

Eighty-nine years later, a thirty-two-year-old astrophysicist will die suddenly, of unknown causes, in the same remote area of the world. He'd been working at a research center named after the explorer; he'd taken a number of exacting tests to ensure his suitability for the rigorous post. He was young, healthy, highly trained, well on his way to becoming an expert. Who would have thought he wouldn't make the cut?

The newspaper account adheres scrupulously to the facts: *Scientist Dies in Isolation.*

No one will make even an educated guess as to why such a condition could kill him until they fly his body back to the city, after the long winter has ended.

Others who almost made it: a group of nineteenth century pioneers, known today for the desperate circumstances that befell them late in a westward journey across the continent that had begun with so much promise.

The catastrophic outcome, in retrospect, seems a textbook example of the notion of *ill-fated*.

Had they listened to experienced travelers, they would never have taken that now-famous wrong fork in the road. Had they arrived at the forsaken mountain pass that bears their name but a day earlier, they might have made it across before the snows began to fall. Had they chosen to stay home, of course, they would never have found themselves at such a pass in the first place.

As it was, they watched helplessly as the drifts piled up to twenty feet or more. They had tried to make their own way across the map and here they were, stymied, on the verge of starvation.

Some of them did unspeakable things to survive.

News of the horrific events spread rapidly and dampened, for a time, a whole nation's appetite for risk. One of the survivors spoke almost obsessively of the experience and was shunned by society; the others, less than half the original number, couldn't find words for what they had witnessed. They just got on with what was left of their lives.

But one woman in the group did her best to keep a record: *I have not wrote you half of the trouble we had, but I have wrote you enough to let you know what trouble is.*

Sometimes, it's the stories themselves that barely survive.


Fact: I saw a ghost today on the subway, he sat next to me as if we'd always traveled together. I knew that profile. The strong jaw, choppy soft brown hair, the pensive stillness of the head.

It was an almost exact likeness of someone I had once known well.

But he's been gone nine years now.

It's striking how tender one can feel toward a stranger, how the slightest reminder takes one's breath away. All of a sudden alternate stories begin to suggest themselves, as if a whole parallel universe of possibilities is still very much in play.

*This is what it would be like if he were still alive, on this ordinary day, on this unremarkable trip uptown.*

I would like to have stopped the train. I wanted to stop time. I knew that once I stepped outside, into the flux of the city, he would be lost to me all over again.

But the train moved on, and so did I.

Like others here, however, I want to keep looking, looking for another glimpse of a ghost.

*Now we need a close, a way to wrap the story up. Maybe something about how the girl we met way back at the beginning grew up, and moved to the city, and looked out her window in wonder, and began to explore her strange surroundings, and soon enough found herself in totally uncharted territory. Maybe something else about how she wishes she had kept her encyclopedia, the one with the bright colorful maps and all that information.*

*But symmetry isn't the answer; city stories resist such easy resolution.*

*No, we need something else, maybe something like this.*

Fact: I am still here. So is the city.

How else could the story have ended?

# Acknowledgments

My first debt is to those anonymous city dwellers who shared, if unwittingly, glimpses into their lives and stories. I also wish to acknowledge the Encyclopedia of New York City for much incidental but fascinating information; The Corporation of Yaddo, PEN American Center, and the PEN/Jerard fund; my editor, Maria Guarnaschelli, and her colleagues at W. W. Norton, who treated this book with the greatest of care; Stanley and Laura Kauffmann; Richard Gilman; Diane Rantanen, Helen Cook, Trevor Harris, and James Nelson; my agent, Georges Borchardt; David Robb, for his wisdom; my friends, particularly Abigail Franklin, Antonio Mercado, Cecilia Rubino, and Dare Clubb; and, of course, the kids.